What Others Are Saying...

"If you and your family are interested in being more effective in supporting Kingdom causes, this book is a valuable tool and a must read."

— David H. Wills, President Emeritus, National Christian Foundation

"To optimize your Kingdom impact, you must ask a different set of planning questions. This book gives you the right questions to ask and then shares a host of true stories of how families and the world have been radically changed when they dared to ask and answer the right planning questions. After reading this book you will not just know more, you will start living differently!"

— E. G. "Jay" Link, Director of Stewardship Planning, Taylor University

"This book will be a blessing to anyone looking to grow in the gift of generosity"

— Todd Harper, Founder and President, Generous Giving

IMPACT

BEST
PRACTICES
of
IMPACT
GIVERS

Published by Generous Impact

ISBN: 978-1-7349559-0-3

Cover Design: Michael Sean Allen
Editor and Interior Design: Jim Armstrong, UpWrite Publishing

20 21 22 23 – 10 9 8 7 6 5 4 3 2 1
1st Printing

Printed in the USA

Contents

IMPACT

Foreword

Early in my Christian life I had two experiences that have profoundly impacted the way I think, believe, and act. The first occurred right after I became a believer. The dentist who was discipling me and I were on the ground floor of a five-story building waiting to get on an elevator. The elevator was almost full when we stepped in. When the doors closed, my mentor asked, "Ron what does Jesus mean to you?" You can imagine the panic that I felt. When we exited on the fifth floor, my mentor said, "Ron, I wanted you to see the value of a thirty-second testimony of your faith."

The second experience came a year or two later. I was on an airplane flying from New York to Los Angeles, and it so happened that I was sitting next to Mike Wallace, the television commentator and much-feared interviewer. As I thought about what I should say to him, I felt the same panic I had felt when I was on the elevator. However, as we flew across the continent, we enjoyed a nice, long conversation, and God gave me the opportunity to share with him my own story. At the end of the flight, his comment to me was, "I believe that you are a reasonably intelligent person, and I cannot argue with your testimony."

What do these stories have to do with this book? That's an easy answer. This book is filled to the brim with personal testimonies of people who have experienced the principles that are highlighted in the book. You can't argue with the illustrations and personal experiences. My friends who have written this book have been in the wealth management business for a long time, working with very wealthy clients, and these stories and testimonies validate what they are teaching.

They share their wisdom and advice using a fourfold approach. First of all, they present the foundational principles that undergird their teaching. Second, they supply the biblical references to support the principles. Third, they furnish the content of what they have experienced and learned; and finally, they provide personal testimonies that support it all. They finish with some very penetrating questions that in reality we all need to answer over and over and over again. Giving and wealth management is a lifelong process or, as they say, a "journey" and not an event.

A financial advisor quoted in the book says, "God cares more about your heart than your money," and another advisor says, "Your giving is a financial expression of your heart for the Kingdom." The Bible says it this way: "Each of you should give what you have decided in your heart to give, not reluctantly or under compulsion for God loves a cheerful giver" (2 Corinthians 9:7). In other words, it is always a heart issue. I know from my years as an advisor and counselor that all behavior is a function of a person's worldview or belief system. Simply put, I can tell where my values truly reside by looking at my checkbook. Where I spend my money is a direct reflection of my heart.

If I could sum up this book, I would say that it is biblical at its core, practical in application, true in example and testimony, authentic in word and wisdom and, lastly, helpful in suggested implementation. The best planning in any area of your financial life is applying the best of financial knowledge with the wisdom of God's Word. Both are contained here, combined in such a way that each of us should be challenged, convicted, and inspired. It has been a privilege for me to read the book, know the authors, and rejoice in the testimonies.

Ron Blue
CEO, Ron Blue Institute
Author and Speaker

Introduction

Why We Wrote This

Wealthy Christians need help! That's why we wrote this book! Over decades of working with generous, wealthy Christians, we have come to an important realization:

There is a deep unmet need in the church for developing the gift of giving in wealthy Christians and their families.

But there is also good news!

"God's Word speaks about wealth and money to every Christian from the wealthiest to the poorest. Whichever you are you should know what it says."

— Pastor Robert Morris,
Gateway Church, Dallas, Texas

As we have heard the stories of countless generous givers, we have discovered some interesting things about generous Christians:

- Becoming a generous giver is mostly self-taught. The average believer receives little education or discipleship in the gift of giving unless they go and look for it. And they often don't know where to look for the resources they need.
- Most conversations about giving happen in relation to a stewardship sermon or capital campaign or as part of a pitch from a ministry to a donor for support. The goals of these conversations are transaction oriented (generate donations for the church or ministry) and not transformational (helping a family learn to be generous towards God). God's Word has a lot to say to wealthy believers and their families, yet they rarely hear it.
- Wealthy Christians often feel isolated. There are few places where believers with surplus wealth can have an honest conversation about their unique needs and challenges.

When God blesses a family with wealth, He also gives them a purpose for that wealth. His plan for them is to find that purpose.

Many wealthy Christian families have a deep hunger to grow in the gift of generosity. They want a deeper understanding of wealth and generosity from a biblical perspective; to understand the special purpose and call God has given them along with their wealth. They want to grow in their faith and help their family members grow closer to Jesus. They want to give effectively to their heartfelt causes, and they want to make a difference. Many are simply searching for the knowledge of how to do it!

The numerous conversations we have had with joyful givers over the years have revealed some core principles that experienced and impactful givers follow that could be helpful to others on their generosity journey.

This book is organized around our nine Best Practices. Impact Givers –

- Have a biblical understanding of wealth and generosity
- Have discovered their purpose
- Understand proportional giving
- Recognize that generosity is a journey
- Form a team
- Give more than cash
- Involve their families in their giving
- Know the difference between success and significance
- Understand legacy

In each chapter focusing on these best practices, you will find the following:

Text: Where we share our views on the importance of each best practice.

Scripture: Where we identify the biblical basis for each of our best practices.

Special guest input: We have been blessed to form friendships with some of the most important and influential people in the generosity community, and we have included some of their insights on each of the best practices.

Points to Ponder: We ask questions that may prod your thinking and encourage you to go deeper into your generosity journey.

Action Plan: We give you an opportunity to write down your plans for implementing these best practices in your own family and personal giving.

We share many personal testimonies in the coming pages. We have changed the names and some of the details to retain anonymity. Otherwise, all the stories are true as presented.

IMPACT

Chapter 1

Biblical Understanding of Wealth and Generosity

"But remember the Lord your God, for it is He who gives you the ability to produce wealth..." (Deuteronomy 8:18a).

"...Be on your guard against all kinds of greed; life does not consist in an abundance of possessions" (Luke 12:15b).

"You will be enriched in every way so that you can be generous on every occasion..." (2 Corinthians 9:11a).

"...God loves a cheerful giver" (2 Corinthians 9:7b).

"Truly I tell you, it is hard for someone who is rich to enter the kingdom of heaven. Again I tell you, it is easier for a camel to go through the eye of a needle than for someone who is rich to enter kingdom of God....With man this is impossible, but with God all things are possible" (Matthew 19:23b, 24, 26b).

"For each believer there are three conversions necessary; the conversion of the heart, the conversion of the mind, and the conversion of the purse."

— Martin Luther

There is probably no other area where worldly advice and biblical advice differ more than about money. Maybe that is why Jesus spoke so often about money and wealth. In fact, He spoke more about money and wealth than about heaven, or prayer! Clearly, He must have been trying to tell us something!

Money is not spiritually neutral. Money has power. That power can be good or bad. Money is a vehicle that moves a soul. Whether it moves our soul or the soul of our family closer to God or further away is largely because of the decisions we make. Certainly, wealth can be wisely used for Kingdom purposes. But we all know families where wealth has ruined the lives of those who possessed it.

The many decisions we make are products of the money thoughts that we have. Most money thoughts are primarily influenced by the culture around us and our family of origin. The culture tells us it's all about us, that we will be happy if we own the right car, live in the right house, take the right vacation. Our family of origin had its own spoken and unspoken views on money, and we largely bought into those whether we realized it or not.

BOTTOM LINE: our views on money have largely been formed unintentionally and not shaped by biblical wisdom.

A biblical view of wealth and generosity is in stark contrast to the worldly view. The Bible says it's not about us, it's about Him! The Bible says we don't own anything; it's all His and we are just temporary managers of the wealth He has entrusted to us. The world says, "He who dies with the most toys wins." Jesus said, "Don't lay up for yourselves treasures on earth; lay up for yourselves treasures in heaven!" (Matthew 6:19-20).

The accumulation of personal wealth is an almost unchallenged goal/belief in our culture. But, if personal wealth is the answer, then why are there so many unhappy wealthy people? In contrast, we have never met an unhappy generous person. What is the connection?

How Much Is Enough?

Luke 12:16-21 —

"And he told them this parable: 'The ground of a certain rich man yielded an abundant harvest. He thought to himself, "What shall I do? I have no place to store my crops."

"'Then he said, "This is what I'll do. I will tear down my barns and build bigger ones, and there I will store my surplus grain. And I'll say to my-

self, 'You have plenty of grain laid up for many years. Take life easy; eat, drink and be merry.'"

"'But God said to him, "You fool! This very night your life will be demanded from you. Then who will get what you have prepared for yourself?"

"'This is how it will be with whoever stores up things for themselves but is not rich toward God.'"

One of the most powerful exercises a Christian family can do is to answer the question, "How much is enough?" Enough is a life-changing financial concept. It is countercultural. In a world where more is always better, enough is a very healthy concept to keep in mind. The Bible clearly warns us about building bigger barns. ***How big is big enough?***

"Enough" helps establish a finish line. Some of the most joyful Christians we know are those who have reached their "enough finish line" and are still working hard, vital and engaged, and using their gifts, talents and results to build God's Kingdom instead of their own.

"Enough" is a stake in the ground demonstrating that, as followers of Jesus, we have different goals and priorities than non-believers.

"Enough" is a great concept in that it is a strategic recognition that the power of money can be either good or bad in a family and needs to be treated as such. It also implies understanding that in some cases more wealth could actually be a bad thing, as counter to culture as that is. History is filled with stories of wealthy families ruining future generations, but few realize that it could happen in their family and that there are biblical warnings to that effect.

Here is a process to follow in setting finish lines. Estimate the total costs involved in you and your spouse maintaining your desired lifestyle, and determine the asset level you will need to support that lifestyle. Estimate the cost of those items you would like to provide for your next generations. Be careful not to overdo your help to the next generations and deprive them of motivation, accomplishment, work, sacrifice and other character-building exercises.

The total of those two numbers (your needs + your heirs' needs) is your "enough number." The rest you are free to use during your lifetime and upon your death to further the great working of the Kingdom here on earth.

Special Guest
Jay Link on Bigger Barns

Wealth comes into a Christian family because someone in the family has the God given ability to generate money far in excess of their needs. Slowly over the years their "barns" fill with assets far beyond anything they had ever imagined. Inevitably, these families face the question: Should they build bigger barns, or does God have a different reason for providing the wealth they enjoy? Based on over 40 years counseling wealthy Christian families, I would like to suggest the following:

1. Don't kill the Golden Goose. If God has given you the gift of creating financial wealth, He gave it to you for a reason! A gift from God is an awesome thing if used wisely! Once you have provided for the needs of your family you have the surplus with which to create a huge Kingdom impact.

2. Do not increase your lifestyle consumption simply because you have an ever-increasing income. It is very easy to get caught in "lifestyle creep": over time the more you have, the more you spend. This type of lifestyle creep happens very gradually, almost unnoticed. What were once luxuries become necessities. Driving becomes flying, coach becomes flying first class, which becomes owning a private jet. *"As goods increase, so do those who consume them"* (Ecclesiastes 5:11a).

    No one should be acting as someone else's lifestyle police. Lifestyle is very personal. The key question to ask ourselves is how much of the wealth God has provided does He want us to keep? God has clearly blessed some families financially. Does He intend them to be a

> bucket or a pipe? A bucket keeps what is poured into it, while a pipe passes it on to others!
>
> 3. Do not keep piling the excess into bigger and bigger barns without a strategy for what to do with it. God told Abraham he had been blessed to be a blessing. The same is true for wealthy Christian families. Handling wealth successfully shouldn't be spontaneous, making it up as you go along. It needs a God-directed plan to bless your family, allowing the power of family money to do more harm than good. Wealthy families have two choices: They can handle their wealth on purpose or by accident. God's purposes don't happen accidentally! Also, many wealth creators really enjoy the process of making money so much that they lose sight of the God-authored purpose for it all. Remember Jesus' admonition, *"What good will it be for someone to gain the whole world, yet forfeit their soul?"* (Matthew 16:26a)

There is a cost to leaving the "How much is enough?" question unanswered. Unrestrained wealth accumulation can lead to emotional bondage regarding money. Emotional financial bondage is a trap, where a person's perceptions of their finances are separated from reality.

During the global financial crisis in 2008, a well-known businessman saw his fortune drop from $2 billion to $1 billion. As a result, he wrote to all the ministries he supported and told them he would be cutting back on his support due to his personal financial crisis. In fact, he cut his giving back to a level significantly below what it was when he "only" had a billion in the past. That's not financial wealth; that's financial bondage.

This is not to be judgmental. It is to point out that because this family didn't have a Kingdom perspective on their wealth, they were unable to joyfully engage their finances when opportunities presented themselves.

Paul's Testimony

A few years back I hosted a couple at a generous giving conference. We sat at a table with a friend of mine who is a well-known philanthropist. One of the speakers talked about how they capped their lifestyle and gave everything over that predetermined amount to Kingdom works.

When the speaker was done, our table was silent for a moment, and then the husband of the couple who were my guests said to the philanthropist at the table, "Did you hear the speaker say that he capped his spending and gave the rest away?"

"Yes," answered my friend.

My guest was quiet for a few moments and then he asked, "Do you know anyone else who does that?"

And my friend the philanthropist said, "Yes."

My guest waited a few more minutes and then said to the philanthropist, "You do that don't you?"

And my friend the philanthropist said, "Yes, my wife and I have done that for many years."

My guest turned to his wife and said, "You know, we could do that."

And she said, "That is what I've been trying to tell you."

And they made a decision on the spot to be more generous. In fact, their giving increased more than fivefold in the years ahead. This was also at the time of the global financial crisis where their net worth dropped by more than 70%!

To this day this couple reminds Paul that becoming radically more generous is one of the best decisions they ever made. It helped them survive an enormous financial setback and enabled their marriage to flourish in adversity.

One of the most valuable resources you can use to help form a biblical understanding of wealth and generosity is *The Treasure Principle* by Randy Alcorn. Although it's a relatively small book, this bestseller has impacted millions of people by explaining the basis for biblical generosity in a powerful way. We can't do the book justice in just a brief summary, but the key principles are as follows:

Treasure Principles

1. God owns everything. I am His money manager.
2. My heart always goes where I put God's money.
3. Heaven—the new earth, not the present one—is my home.
4. I should live not for the dot (representing today) but for the line (representing eternity).
5. Giving is the antidote to materialism.
6. God prospers me not to raise my standard of living but to raise my standard of giving.

All of this serves to remind us, "You can't take it with you, but you can send it on ahead."

We encourage you to read *The Treasure Principle* as a great foundation for your generosity journey.

False Prophets

We would like to go on record as saying that we believe "prosperity theology" is a false gospel. We believe it is a distortion of the teachings of Jesus. Yes, God wants to bless us and reward our generosity. But God is more interested in eternity than the here and now. And a "god" who can only bless with material wealth is too small to be the God of the Bible. Over our years as givers, God has rewarded us in countless ways—especially by blessing us with an incredible group of generous people to share the journey and, a few times, even a glimpse of eternal rewards.

God can bless us in ways far bigger than money. Anyone who is looking for money from Him needs to enlarge his or her idea of God! Also, to paraphrase Randy Alcorn, prosperity theology is errant theology, because a true theology has to be as true in New York City and Beverly Hills as it is in rural India or a garbage dump in Brazil.

? Points to Ponder

1. How much is enough for you? Your family?
   What should you do with the rest?

2. What core beliefs about money and wealth do you need to
   re-examine in light of biblical principles?

3. Where did your wealth come from?

4. When you give, do you feel you are gaining or losing?

➡ Action Plan

1. Read *The Treasure Principle* (as a family or couple).

2. Include growing in biblical financial wisdom in our prayer
   time.

Write your unique action items in the spaces provided below:

3. _____

   _____

4. _____

   _____

5. _____

   _____

Chapter 2

Impact Givers Discover Their Purpose

"Command those who are rich in this present world not to be arrogant nor to put their hopes in wealth, which is so uncertain, but to put their hope in God, who richly provides us with everything for our enjoyment. Command those to do good, to be rich in good deeds, and to be generous and willing to share. In that they will lay up treasure for themselves as a firm foundation for the coming age, so that they may take hold of the life that is truly life" (1 Timothy 6:17-19).

"For what Kingdom purpose did God entrust you with all this wealth?"

— Henry Blackaby
author, theologian

Henry Blackaby's question is a challenging one for wealthy Christians. It challenges the unspoken assumption that our wealth is ours because we earned it; we get to keep it and decide how it's spent, including how much we will give or "tithe" to Kingdom works.

Here are some facts from a biblical perspective:

- As Pastor Rick Warren says, "It's not about you!" It's not about your stuff, your comfort or your wealth. God gave you your wealth and your ability to earn for His purposes, not yours.

- The Bible tells us, *"To whom much is given, from him much will be required"* (Luke 12:48 NKJV). Wealthy believers need to search and find their personal passion for some area (or areas) of Kingdom work that compels them to gladly spend their time and money. Some people are grabbed by church planting or evangelism or saving babies from abortion. Others are focused on orphans, adoption and children at risk or church planting. God gives a purpose for our wealth, and we are expected to find it.

We believe God gave you the wealth and you the purpose and you the responsibility for how you handle your wealth. As Ron Blue says, "Money is a tool, a test and a testimony." Your wealth is a tool that God has given you to build His Kingdom. It is a test of your spiritual maturity. It is a testimony for you to write! You can't delegate it to others. It's your responsibility. God has given you the challenge of wealth to help you grow! You are expected to be pro-active, responsible stewards over the funds that have been entrusted to you. Your role is not passive! Your giving decisions are not to be made by your pastor or development people or fund-raising officers or ministries or a televangelist that would like your support or well-intended friends and acquaintances. Each of these people, especially your pastor, may be able to play an important role in your journey, but it's your journey, not theirs! They will not ultimately be called to account for what you did with the wealth you were given, you will.

Too often, the only money conversation wealthy Christians have is about a donation. In effect, churches and missions feel they have the vision and wealthy Christians have the money to fund the vision. But wealthy Christians should develop their own vision for building the Kingdom and then work with partners to make the vision a reality! One of the most important goals of this chapter's Best Practices exercise is to help you move as much as possible toward hearing, "Well done, good and faithful servant" with regards to your giving (see Matthew 5:21).

Finding your purpose may be easy or it may be really hard work. But it is a critical first step. Purpose leads to passion. Passion leads to impact!

In 2002, Pastor Rick Warren wrote a book called *The Purpose Driven Life*. It became the second most translated non-fiction book after the Bible. Much of its popularity was due to its deep connection to the question on the hearts of many Christians, "What is my purpose? What on earth am I here for?" The question is important in your generosity journey. Once you have identified your purpose, your giving should be part of that purpose. Makes sense, right?

Pastor Rick developed a simple model for helping us understand our purpose. It's called S.H.A.P.E. Here is how it applies to our giving:

- **Spiritual Gifts:** The Bible tells us we are all given spiritual gifts. Those gifts get stronger as we exercise them just like physical exercise builds muscle. Giving helps us exercise the gift/muscle of generosity.

- **Heart:** God has given you a heart for the areas where He wants you to be generous. Many believers base their giving on the emotions that they feel when they are asked for money. But we believe that God has also put in your heart something that moves you in a unique way. What brings tears to your eyes? If there was one problem in the world you could solve what would it be? That is the Holy Spirit directing your heart towards God's plan for your giving.

- **Abilities:** God will give you the abilities to execute the plan He has given you. But He won't necessarily give them in advance!

- **Personality:** God gave you your personality along with your purpose. They go together.

- **Experience:** Our experiences over time become a rich reservoir to draw on for wisdom and application. Your experience as a coach prepared you to be a mentor. Your experience as a parent prepared you to be a foster parent. Your experience as a carpenter prepared you to build houses for those in need of shelter. Generally, God gives you assignments that grow out of your experience, and God wisely gives us a passion for what He assigns us.

God will give you a purpose and a calling consistent with your shape. Years ago, Jack held a retreat for 50 businessmen in his church. During that weekend 48 felt they should consider leaving their professional life to "serve the Lord in full-time ministry."

What's wrong with this picture? Surely a few could be called to the mission field, but all of them? These men didn't need a new profession, they needed a new paradigm! God could use them right where they already were, if they just made their professional career about Him! There are numerous ministries that can help equip laypeople to develop their Kingdom-directed calling right in the business environment where God has placed them. Those men needed to see that God could use them, their gifts and talents right where He already had them, to grow where they were placed.

Giving with a purpose is strategic, not emotional. Many people mistake emotion for generosity. But responding to a presented need like a national disaster or a "flies in the eyes" child sponsorship commercial is only a small part of generosity. Much more significant is the dedicated, committed, pre-planned allocation of family wealth and income over time to Kingdom works. Consistently long-term giving to well-thought-out and prayed-over causes is likely to be more impactful than sporadic impulsive gifts to needs that arise.

Giving with a purpose is planned in advance, strategic and impactful, the result of a process where all of the best practices of impact givers are included. Purposeful, impactful giving is personal. It grows from a deep place in your faith and expresses itself in a very personal way. Your giving is a financial expression of your heart for the Kingdom. Your giving plan should be as personal as your devotion time, your prayer time, your retirement and estate plans.

Most serious givers do not delegate their giving decisions to others. Many inexperienced givers have no real giving plan, and their giving is mostly done as a response to a stewardship message, or capital campaign or development office visit. Many, many generous believers can become exhausted by the endless requests for money they receive. The remedy for this situation is for your family to decide in advance whom you will give to and why. Once you have prayerfully and strategically decided whom to give to, you can easily say "no" to others who may ask for support. No one can say "yes" to every ask. A purposeful personal giving plan can help you with your "yeses" and "noes." Our experience with wealthy generous families is that they don't give based on being asked (reactive), but they follow a plan (proactive). Having a plan makes it easy to say yes to those opportunities that fit the plan and no to ones that don't.

Mitch, a businessman, recently lamented that he found giving to be a bad experience. It wasn't parting with the money that bothered him. As a member of a very high profile family, he was constantly being "hit up" for donations.

A friend wisely counseled, "Do you want to know how to make it more joyful? Create your own family giving plan. Seek God's plan and purpose for your giving. Be as proactive in your giving as you are in your business. Decide where you want to give and say no to everything else."

"Can I do that?" he asked, as a completely new paradigm emerged in his thinking.

"Of course you can. In fact, you should. It gives you focus and removes the guilt."

Counsel from CJ, a well-known advisor and philanthropist

It is critically important that each generous family prayerfully work through their foundational beliefs about tithing and giving. It is not enough to copy someone else's beliefs; you need to work to develop and own yours. God cares more about your heart than your money. This process of forming your own beliefs will cause you to grow in your faith. My core beliefs about tithes are as follows:

1. God is not an accountant. He looks into the heart.
2. We should give significantly to our local church but not necessarily exclusively. If you have legitimate reasons to not want to support your church financially, this may be a sign that you should be looking for a new church. Otherwise, your local church is your first financial obligation.
3. The tithe is Old Testament. New Testament giving is in response to a God who gave His life for us. Our response should be far beyond the 10% level.
4. There are many valid interpretations of what the storehouse is today. Ideally your church is deserving of your support, but God may put a heavier burden on your family's heart for other causes beyond the local church. You should joyfully answer either call. And ideally, your pastor should be supportive. Clearly, God wants the local church to succeed. Just as clearly, He wants us supporting and involved in the wonderful works around the world done by parachurch ministries.
5. God places a special burden on some families and gives them the resources for that burden. The details vary greatly and often don't follow a formula.

Fred was a very successful young businessman who God allowed to sell his business for a substantial sum. Rather than give the money away, he invested in such a way as to provide for his family and has over the last 30 years been financially free to serve in ministry for a far-below-market salary and has had international impact in his work.

Carl was making $10 million a year when he got saved. His church had a budget under $1 million. When his pastor told him his $1 million tithe belonged to the local church, he wisely replied, "Pastor, my tithe would ruin your church!" Carl gave generously to his local church, but also formed a family foundation that has focused on worldwide evangelism and has had a powerful impact.

Ray is a friend who is a serial inventor-entrepreneur. He has countless patents to his name. He regularly invents things, builds a business around the invention, sells the business, gives the money away and starts again.

These are amazing God-honoring strategies. None is "right for everyone." It's personal and isn't related to tithing at all. These believers are far beyond the tithe and loving it!

From a real-world standpoint, the vast majority of wealthy Christian families are generous supporters of their local churches, but the majority of their giving goes to other causes. Often, they use a private foundation or family giving fund. The relationship between your local church/pastor and your giving is something that needs to be worked out prayerfully as a family. There are no biblically set rigid rules. Of course, you should respect your pastor's authority. At the same time there is no one size fits all solution. It's not about accounting, it's about obedience.

Testimony:
The Campions

When Don Campion saw the Egbe Hospital again, he knew he had to do something. This missionary hospital in Nigeria had been founded by his parents five decades earlier. Returning in 2008 with his wife SueAnn to show her his childhood home, he found the hospital in a state of disrepair and collapse. He knew in his heart this could not stand.

Nigeria was a long way from Don's life in South Florida. Starting as a worker at the local airport, Don used his skills developed in Africa working on the missionary planes to start a jet service company that has grown to be one of the top companies of its type in South Florida. With a renewed passion in his heart for his parents' hospital legacy, Don and SueAnn began to pull together the network and resources to restore and revitalize Egbe Hospital. They have been able to call upon their network here in the U.S. as well as their own personal resources to fund the work. Many of Don's childhood friends in Nigeria are now tribal and community leaders who are facilitating the work on the ground. Today Egbe Hospital serves over 1,000 patients a month in an area that otherwise has no hospital facilities. Egbe Hospital is a living testimony to the impact one family with purpose and passion can have.

Testimony:
Patricia

The night Patricia went to the movies the last thing she expected was a life-changing experience. Life for Patricia was good. She and her husband had built one of the most successful businesses in their Central American country. Their usual companions were other wealthy and powerful countrymen. The poverty of her country was far removed from her day-to-day life—until that night in 1995. Leaving the theater, Patricia was approached by two young boys under 10 asking for food or money. As she talked with them she heard a baby's cry. The boys took her into a nearby alley where their baby sister lay in a wood crate. Her heart broke. "This can't be!" she screamed inside. On that spot God birthed a vision to provide a safe environment for children in her country to live and grow towards adulthood. At first the children were housed by ones and twos in various locations in the capital city. Eventually, Patricia partnered with World Vision and U.S. donors to build a children's home called Fundación Exodo. Today over 50 children live in the homes on a mountainside overlooking the Pacific. They receive medical and mental health care, education and vocational training, as well as having a safe place to spend their childhood. Exodo exemplifies what can happen when a believer listens and acts on God's call on his or her life.

In God's Kingdom, wealth with purpose is a powerful combination. Wealth without purpose is rarely fulfilling. Travis made over a hundred million dollars selling his chain of steak restaurants. He recalled, "For nine months I did everything rich guys are supposed to do. I flew all over the world by private jet. I ate every delicacy and had every spa treatment you can name. It was the most boring nine months of my life."

Years ago **George** had a room in a beach house in the Hamptons for a summer. One of the roommates was best friend to a young man whose father was Chairman of one of Wall Street's top firms. Anyone on Wall Street would know his name. George noticed that when Junior visited, he called Senior multiple times a day and spoke very briefly. The reason was that Senior had a really hard time handling life when the office was closed and out of concern for his well-being, some family member or friend called him hourly from 5:00 p.m. Friday until Monday morning every week! Without the work environment, he was lost!

Even in the secular world, wealth needs a purpose. Many times God will use a Bible verse or an event or a person to bring our purpose and calling to mind. The heart of one family's giving has been toward orphans. **Derek**, the father, received a Bible verse identifying this calling at a conference several years ago when Rich Stearns from World Vision was the speaker. He mentioned his life verse and immediately upon hearing it, it became Derek's also.

It was Job 29:11-12, 16, *"Whoever heard me spoke well of me, and those who saw me commended me, because I rescued the poor who cried for help and the fatherless who had none to assist them.... I was a father to the needy; I took up the case of the stranger."* All Derek needed was to hear those words and he knew that they would have a special place in his heart.

God has also given one family a story that is not only true but a parable for our giving purpose. Their daughter was born in China many years ago. For reasons we cannot know, she was left on the steps of an orphanage in the night. When she was found by a groundskeeper at dawn the next day, she was already suffering from hypothermia and was extremely ill. She was brought inside and examined, as was their intake process at the time. Because she was so ill, it was determined that she could not be saved and that scarce resources for the other children could not be allocated to her care. She was placed in a basket and left to be taken to the expiration room. While she was there, the director of the orphanage passed by, took one look at her and exclaimed, "Why is this child in this line? We need to move her. She must be saved. Look at her face! This child is of the Ming Dynasty. This child has the blood of royalty. This child has the face of a king."

So the baby girl was moved from the line that leads to death and placed in the line that leads to life. Months later she was adopted into her family, where she has thrived and made the world a glowing better place. And that story burned itself into their hearts and leads their giving. There are children all over the world that, through no cause of their own, are in a line that leads to death and destruction. By partnering with ministries they are trying to move as many as they can from the line that leads to death to the line that leads to life. because every one of them has royal blood in their veins, every one of them has the face of a King.

❓ *Points to Ponder*

1. Why do you give where you give?

2. Do you sense a calling to a specific area of Kingdom work?

3. What area of ministry has your life experience prepared you for?

4. If money were no obstacle, what great problem would you solve?

5. Do you have a life verse? How does it relate to your giving?

➡️ *Action Plan*

1. Begin to pray and ask God for a revelation for His purpose in my wealth.

2. Schedule some time with passionate givers and ask them how they discovered their purpose.

Write your unique action items in the spaces provided below:

3. _____

_____

IMPACT

4. _____

   _____

5. _____

   _____

Chapter 3

Proportional Giving

"...From everyone who has been given much, much will be demanded; and from the one who has been entrusted with much, much more will be asked" (Luke 12:48b).

"Now finish the work, so that your eager willingness to do it may be matched by your completion of it, according to your means" (2 Corinthians 8:11).

"On the first day of every week, each one of you should set aside a sum of money in keeping with your income, saving it up, so that when I come no collections will to be made" (1 Corinthians 16:2).

Maybe you heard about the guy who won $3 million in the lottery and said he was going to give a quarter of it to charity. Now, he just has to decide what to do with the other $2,999,999.75.

Dennis and Allison

In 2004, Dennis and Allison were making New Year's resolutions. They weren't normally big on resolutions, but this year was different. They had both sensed that they needed to increase their giving from the basic tithe. Their income was growing, but so were their expenses. They had just read Randy Alcorn's *Money, Possessions, and Eternity* and were really impacted by the section on giving. God had blessed them, and they wanted to be a blessing to others. Not wanting to influence each other, they prayed separately and asked God to reveal to them how much He wanted them to give. They both felt God

33

told them to give 15%, so they did. As God would have it, in that next year, their income grew by more than the "extra" 5% they gave. So, the next year, they prayed again and they both felt led to give 20%. They did that for a year.

Then, they read Randy Alcorn's book, *The Treasure Principle*, and it really struck a chord. While there are six keys in the book, there are two that really stood out to them:

1. Giving is the only antidote to materialism.
2. God prospers me not to raise my standard of living, but to raise my standard of giving.

They began to sense that God was calling them to cap their lifestyle. They didn't really know what that meant, because they had never met anyone who had done this. What they sensed was that they had more than they needed and God was entrusting them to share His resources. When Dennis told Allison about this, he was worried what she might say, but his concern was unnecessary. The only question she had was, "How do we do that?" He told her he didn't know because he didn't know anyone who did this. So, they rewrote their budget and went from there. And since 2006, that's just what they've done. They want to be clear that they don't live like paupers. But, they do live well below the lifestyle they could be living. What some may see as restrictive has actually been quite freeing. They've really embraced the idea that it isn't about how much we give to God. It's really about how much He lets us keep.

Seriously, generous givers are not well served by the usual talk about money in the church. Tithing, pledges, and stewardship are words that address financial giving but do not reflect the excitement of having a generous heart. Determining how much to give includes financial calculations, but it shouldn't be limited by formulas. Generosity can include tithing and stewardship, but it is so much more. Generosity helps define our relationship with God and exemplifies our priorities.

Wouldn't it make sense that those with large amounts of surplus wealth would have a greater responsibility to be generous than those who are struggling? Clearly it is a very different level of sacrifice for someone to tithe from a $20,000 income than from a $2 million income. Is tithing from a large income really a sacrifice? Not if you consider Who allowed you that wealth to begin with!

Money and giving are areas where our beliefs and attitudes can actually be measured. Billy Graham often said if you want to know where person's heart is just take a look at their checkbook. No person can tell another what their giving level should be. The exciting part about this process is that it goes to the heart of a believer's relationship with God. Generous givers need trust, faith, Kingdom hearts and eternal perspectives!

There are no magic formulas for how much to give. The perfect amount to give is the amount God asks you to give. At its best, giving is about relationship, not rules. Many wealthy and generous Christians have long left the tithe behind and are giving far beyond those levels. They arrive at their own personal giving plan based on thoughtful and prayerful consideration of what God expects of them. Their giving is guided by their personal relationship with Christ. Sometimes those giving levels can rise to 50% of income—even 90%. Some wealthy Christian families have decided to cap their spending each year and give away all of their income above that amount.

We know of several wealthy families who could live an extravagant lifestyle but choose not to. Even though they make millions of dollars annually, they cap their spending at a level well below that and give all the remaining earnings away. That is radical!

Another strategy being adopted by generous givers is to set a finish line number. A family might determine that $3 million or $5 million or $50 million net worth is their "finish line." They give away everything above that number. So if a family has determined their finish line to be $10 million, every year they try to give away whatever they accumulate above that amount no matter how much it is.

These are all creative ways to implement a common underlying strategy: They are more interested in increasing their giving than increasing their lifestyle. Generous giving is based on a heart monitor, not a calculator.

Ron Blue describes a solid giving strategy consisting of three elements:

Should give: Every Christian is expected to be financially supportive of God's work while here on earth. The starting point traditionally is the tithe, which represents 10% of income. One thing we have learned is that getting started giving is the hardest part. The first small checks we wrote were much harder than much larger checks we wrote later.

Zack remembers when he was a new Christian and his pastor explained the tithe to him. He was making $50,000 a year and a tithe was $5,000! That seemed impossible! He couldn't live on the rest. What he didn't realize was God could make the 90% go further than he ever could with the 100%. He wrote a check for $500 and put it in the offering plate on Sunday. By Wednesday he had called the church three times to find out how the money had been spent! Soon after, the pastor called him and told him he didn't understand that when he gave an offering it's not his money anymore and if he called about it again he was going to give him a refund! He survived the pain of that first gift and many thereafter. God has done more with his treasure and talents than he ever could have, just as God has promised.

Could give: Many Christians can give more than 10% if they are willing to sacrifice and make generosity more of a priority than current lifestyle. Sacrificial giving is giving up something we would like to spend money on (vacations, second homes, airplanes) in order to give more to the Lord's work.

Could give is a real challenge. Could give involves a conscious decision to sacrifice things we would enjoy for ourselves to invest in things of the Kingdom. Could give involves a sacrifice of lifestyle and enjoyment for a greater participation in Kingdom activities. Could give is hard work and challenging. It also builds generosity and spiritual growth.

Would give: This is a faith gift. It is a pre-commitment to make a gift from an amount of money that is currently not available. As an example, would give says that if God provides a windfall, such as a bonus, raise or inheritance, all of that money will be given away. This is an exercise of faith and trust and supernatural appointments.

Rick Warren, speaking at a Generous Giving conference, gave a great example of "would give." Saddleback, his church, met for about 15 years in rented facilities. Eventually the day came to buy land and build a campus, and a capital campaign was set up. Rick and his wife prayed about how much to personally give. Independently they arrived at the same amount: two times his $75,000 a year salary, or $150,000. That Sunday, Rick announced to the congregation that, when they gathered in four weeks to make their pledges, the Warrens had committed to $150,000 and they had no money in the bank and no idea where it would come from.

Three and a half weeks passed. The Thursday before pledge Sunday, with no money to meet the pledge and no idea where it could come from, Rick got a call. A publisher asked him if he would be willing to write a book based on his teachings about The Purpose Driven Church. They were willing to pay him an advance of, you guessed it, $150,000! Rick went to Saddleback three days later and told his congregation, "I got the money!" His "would give" example was a huge inspiration to his church, allowing them to see faith in action in the area of generosity.

This next story belongs in the "believe it or not" category, but we have verified it with people who attend the church.

About ten years ago a new church on Long Island was bursting at the seams and needed a new building in which to meet. The leadership committed to not go into debt to buy a building. They agreed to collect money over a set period of time, and only proceed with the purchase if they had enough for a cash purchase. At the end of the announcement the pastor joked that he would accept cash, checks, credit cards and winning lottery tickets if anyone was so inclined.

A short time later, in the offering plate there was an anonymous envelope containing a winning $1 million lottery ticket. The anonymous donor didn't give a tithe—they gave it all, just like Jesus did.

Extravagantly satisfying joyful giving is not the product of a formula. God's giving level is not found by math, it's found by prayer. Generous givers continually try to find ways to give more, not less. Giving is something they get to do, not something they have to do.

Sam

Sam is a very high earner and very generous. As he approaches retirement, he is very troubled that a substantial drop in income will lead to a substantial drop in giving.

A major financial priority for Sam and his wife is to continue their giving and having a Kingdom impact in their retirement years.

Here is how the conversation went between Sam and his financial advisor:

FA: Have you considered structuring your giving in a new way?

Sam: How?

FA: How much money do you think you and your wife will need to live comfortably in retirement?

Sam: $200k a year.

FA: That takes $5 million invested @ 4%. You already have that and you aren't retiring for 7 years or more.

Sam: Okay.

FA: So why don't you and your wife agree to cap your portfolio at $5 million, cap your lifestyle at $200k a year and give the rest away? So, if you start the year with $5 million and you end with $5.5 million you give $500k away. Just like that.

Sam was blown away by this new idea; simple and straightforward. He has incorporated it into this long-term plan and is thrilled that they can continue his philanthropy into this retirement years.

Trevor

Trevor once shared a simple, elegant, joyful giving plan; Every year he and his wife make sure they give more to Kingdom works than they spend on themselves! What a great God-first approach!

Dugan

When Dugan got saved, one of the first things his pastor taught him was the importance of biblical generosity, and specifically the tithe. At that time he was making $70,000 a year. Giving $7,000 annually seemed crazy. It took about two years to get to the tithe level but he got there. Over time his income doubled to $150,000 and since that was more than double the average income in our country, his wife and he agreed to 20% annual giving, plus above that amount as the call presented. They also made lifetime goal of $1 million in Kingdom giving, which seemed impossible at the time. They hit the goal in about 10 years and hit $2 million about eight years later. Currently they are closing in on $4 million in lifetime giving and can easily foresee doubling that amount in their lifetime. R. J. LeTourneau* said when asked about his 90% giving, "I shovel my money to God and He shovels His blessings towards me.

God's shovel is bigger than mine!"

Recently Dugan had the opportunity to sell his business. The sale price was more than all their lifetime giving combined. God truly has a bigger shovel. Dugan recently said, "One of the most important lessons we learned is that Kingdom giving is something we get to do, not something that we have to do."

*R. J. LeTourneau was a pioneer in the heavy equipment industry. His story is told in the book, Mover of Men and Mountains. He regularly gave 90% of his income to Kingdom works.

Tithing

One of the most discussed topics in giving is the concept of tithing. Serious debatable questions arise. Is the tithe still operative (New Testament or Old Testament)? Is the tithe all that is required? Is the tithe to the local church?

Larry Burkett is the father of our modern biblical view of money and finances. Howard Dayton, Ron Blue and Dave Ramsey all flow out of Larry's foundational work in this area. Here is what he has to say about the tithe.

The Tithe
By Larry Burkett

In Psalm 24 David declares, *"The earth is the Lord's, and all it contains"* (NASB). In 1 Corinthians 4:7 the apostle Paul asks, *"What do you have that you did not receive?"* (NASB) And in Deuteronomy 8:18, God told the Jews that He was the one giving them the power to make wealth.

From these verses alone, it should be obvious that God owns everything, gives us the ability to make a living, and wants us to recognize that everything comes from Him.

We simply are stewards, or managers, of the things He has entrusted to us, and part of being a good steward is giving back to God a portion of our earnings.

It's not that God needs our money. Rather, giving serves as an external, material testimony that God owns both the material and spiritual things of our lives.

The history of giving

As early as the book of Genesis, we find Abraham giving something called a "tithe" to the priest Melchizedek. In Hebrew, the word tithe is *maaser* and in the Greek it's *dekate*. But the literal meaning of both words is "tenth."

Abraham tithed in Genesis 14 after returning from the rescue of his nephew Lot from four enemy kings. When he encountered Melchizedek, he voluntarily surrendered to him one-tenth of all the spoils he had taken from his enemies.

People sometimes argue that the tithe was part of the Mosaic Law and doesn't apply to modern-day Christians, who are not under the law. But Abraham tithed some 430 years before the Law was given to Moses.

Furthermore, even in the days of Moses, the tithe was not a law. Although it appears in the legal book of Leviticus (chapter 27), there is no punishment associated with the failure to tithe. However, there is a consequence: loss of blessings.

How much is a tithe?

I believe that giving was meant to be individualized, even in Moses' time. It never was intended that everyone should give the same but that each should give according to his or her abundance and conviction (see 1 Corinthians 16:2, 2 Corinthians 9:7).

One-tenth was the minimum standard, but the book of Deuteronomy lists several additional offerings described as tithes of a person's increase. Thus, it's likely that those who could gave much more than 10 percent in those days.

Couples who cannot commit a tenth of their resources to God should realistically examine their spending and living habits.

Where should the tithe go?

According to Malachi 3:10, the tithe was supposed to be brought into the storehouse, which was a place where the Jews delivered their offerings of grain or animals.

The storehouse had specific functions, including feeding the tribe of Levi (numbers 18:24-29), Feeding the Hebrew widows and orphans living within the Hebrew city (Deuteronomy 14:28-29), and feeding the Gentile poor living in the Hebrew city (Deuteronomy 14:28-29).

Ideally, the local church could serve as the storehouse in God's economy today. God has designed the church to carry out vital social functions similar to those funded by the storehouse. Churches also should minister to the sick, teach families to care for themselves, and take the Gospel to the lost at home and abroad.

Some churches do not minister fully in these areas. Therefore, to the extent that a church lacks in a specific area of ministry, a portion of the tithe could be given to an individual or organization that is "filling in the gap." However, remember that you cannot sit under the teaching of a local church without supporting it financially (see 1 Timothy 5:17-18).

What if my spouse disagrees?

One of the major causes of arguments among couples is money, and one spouse may oppose giving a tenth to God's work. However, if both spouses are Christians, they should have a desire to please the Lord.

It's important for both spouses to be trained in God's principles of finance. That way, they'll understand that tithing is ordained by God, not just a personal desire that the wife is trying to impose on the husband, or vice versa.

In cases involving a non-Christian wife, the husband must obey the Lord's direction. He must realize, however, that the Lord is more concerned about his wife's soul than his money. If tithing becomes a stumbling block to his wife, he should consider not tithing temporarily in order to win his wife to the Lord.

If the non-Christian spouse is the husband, then the believing wife should submit to his wishes, trusting that her submissive attitude may win him to the Lord (1 Peter 3:1-6). She may still ask him to let her give an amount smaller than the tithe for at least a year. If, at the end of a year, they are worse off financially as a result of her giving, she will cease to give. But if they are better off, she will be allowed to give more.

In Malachi 3:10, the Lord says to test Him in tithing. Often, this is just the opportunity for God to prove Himself to an unbelieving spouse.

Gross or net?

There appears to be some confusion as to whether we should calculate our tithe based on our gross incomes (before taxes and other deductions) or net incomes (after taxes and other deductions).

According to Proverbs 3:9-10, God has asked for our first fruits, which is the first and best of all that we receive.

Therefore, we should tithe from our gross, or total, income before taxes. When we calculate our tithes based on net income, we put the government ahead of God.

? Points to Ponder

1. How do we decide how much to give?

2. When was the last time you made the decision to increase your giving?

   What caused you to make that decision?

3. What holds you back from giving more?

4. What is your should give?

   Could give?

   Would give?

⇨ Action Plan

1. As a couple/family, we will determine our should give, could give and would give.

2. Explore the tithing issue and how it relates to our family.

Write your unique action items in the spaces provided below:

3. _____

   _____

4. _____

   _____

5. _____

   _____

Chapter 4

Generosity Is a Journey

"Each of you should give what you have decided in your heart to give, not reluctantly or under compulsion, for God loves a cheerful giver" (2 Corinthians 9:7).

"Religion that God our Father accepts as pure and faultless is this: to look after orphans and widows in their distress and to keep oneself from being polluted by the world" (James 1:27).

George's Story

When George was 24 years old, he had a very good job with a small financial planning firm. He started working there when he was 16 years old after being laid off from a restaurant that summer. His initial job at the firm was making copies and other menial tasks. He always thought his destiny was to go from the copy room to the boardroom. But, God was calling him to something else. He was always impressed by Larry Burkett and Ron Blue and felt led to become a financial planner that focused on biblical principles. He was an operations guy at the time and not really looking to be a financial planner.

He met another financial advisor who was looking for a "young guy" to help him out. The salary he promised was $0. He would keep half of the commissions/fees he generated, which was a little better than what the average advisor received. He was making $40,000 per year at the time.

He wanted to leave on great terms with his firm. George had worked there eight years and had a great rapport with his bosses and co-workers. He had moved from "copy boy" to operations manager. He gave six weeks' notice. George still remembers the lump he had in his throat when he told his boss. These people had really become like family, but God made it very clear that He was calling him to make this move.

About two weeks before he left, one of the executives called George to his office and told him they wanted him to stay and would pay him $50,000/year. He politely declined and told him he wasn't leaving to make more money. His salary was actually going to be $0. The next day, another executive called George in and asked him to stay and that he was authorized to pay him $60,000 a year. Again, George politely declined. He told his wife about this offer and she asked, "What if they offer you six figures?" He said, "There's no way they'll do that. I'm only 24 years old." (Spoiler alert: She was right!)

The next day, the first executive came back to him and said, "You're really driving a hard bargain." He proceeded to offer him $70,000 per year. George told him he wasn't negotiating. He was literally telling the truth. George again politely declined.

The next day, the owner of the company came in and took George to his yacht club and put on the full court press. At one point, he took him to the dock and showed him one of his yachts and told George that if he kept working hard, he could have a life like this. Little did he know that this wasn't attractive to George. This experience reminded him of Jesus being tempted by the devil in Matthew 4 (and Luke 4). Not that he thought he was Jesus, and the owner certainly wasn't the devil.

When they came back to his office, he told George that he was willing to "overpay" him at this stage in his career and that next year, if he kept up the hard work, he'd be a Vice President making six figures. He couldn't believe it! He wanted to tell him "No!" He didn't want to be tempted to stay for the money. He felt God had called him to this other career and he was ready to go. But then doubt started creeping in: What if

God was using this other job offer to replace my income and my wife's income so that we could start a family?

The owner sent George home, who promptly called his wife at work. When she answered, he said, "They offered me six figures like you said. Not today, but next year." The first words out of her mouth were, "You said no, didn't you?" George told her that the owner wouldn't let him but that her words confirmed for him what he needed to do. So, he went in that Monday and declined their generous offer.

For the first year or so, he often regretted that decision. It took George six weeks to earn his first paycheck and it was $50.64. He "quit" many times in that first year and not many times fewer the second year, but eventually he got his footing and he has been in business now for 20 years.

Biblical generosity is a journey, not a transaction. God uses our interaction with money as a tool to shape us and help us grow closer to Him. It is more about relationship than money. Generosity is a gift we can measure and cultivate. We can measure financial generosity easily by counting how much we give and comparing it to our income and resources. We can measure if our generosity has stagnated or grown over time. In giving as in other areas of our faith walk, God loves us right where we are, but He loves us too much to leave us there.

We can cultivate our gift of generosity by using the resources available to us to help us grow. We should recognize that we are not all at the same place on the journey. We need to understand where we are and then use resources appropriate to our situation to learn and grow. Some of us are beginners in giving; others are more experienced and mature. If you were interested in becoming a doctor, you wouldn't apply to medical school if you hadn't completed the undergraduate work necessary to qualify. So too in giving—you need to start in the right place based on your gifting and experience.

There is a radical difference between those who understand wealth from a biblical standpoint and those who don't.

Miles and Stephanie inherited several million dollars while in their 20s. She was a stay-at-home mom and he was a schoolteacher. When we met them, Miles immediately asked, "As Christians, should we tithe on this money?" He then told us they were graduates of a Crown Financial Ministries class, and even though they had never seen an amount like their six figure tithe before, they were committed to it.

Brad was a development officer for one of the country's largest ministries. Many years ago a young couple from the Southwest had a windfall of over $100 million from taking a company public. Brad visited them with a proposal to fund a $5 million giving fund to support poor kids in Mexico, which was the husband's passion. After a careful detailed presentation, the husband was all in. But the wife said, "I would really like to but I don't think we can afford to do it. School starts next month and our (3) girls all need new shoes."

Understanding God's purpose for your wealth makes a big difference.

Special Guest Interview: Todd Harper

Todd Harper is a dear friend and the President of Generous Giving, (affectionately known as GG). GG is a not-for-profit organization whose sole purpose is to provide resources to wealthy Christian families to help them experience the unexpected joy of biblical generosity. The cornerstone of their work is their annual Generous Giving conference where 500+ wealthy believers meet to share about generosity and giving. Over the years Todd has spent countless hours in fellowship and conversation with some of the wealthiest Christian families in the world.

Us: Todd, you have had a great deal of experience over the last years with wealthy Christian families. What have you learned?

TH: Christians who have been blessed with wealth are hungry for wisdom about how to handle the blessings and challenges of their wealth. They are hungry for a peer conversation. With peers they feel safe. They don't have to be embarrassed or self-conscious about their financial success. They like to be with others who get it—that having more wealth than they need is a blessing, but it can also derail them from what is most important to them.

Us: What message does the Bible have for wealthy Christians today?

TH: There are more than twenty-three hundred verses in the Bible about money. Jesus spoke more about money than any other topic. He said more about money than about heaven or hell. There's more written in the Bible about money than written about prayer and faith combined. Clearly money is a big deal to God, so the question all of us who love Him have to address is, "Do I really believe what the Bible teaches about money, and if so, what am I going to do about it?"

So what does the Bible actually say about money? Lots But its message could be summarized with a couple of simple sentences: Be careful. Be generous. Be careful because earthly success could equal spiritual failure, a warning Jesus offers in the Parable of the Rich Fool (Luke 12:21). The best way to be careful is to hold your money loosely—be generous. And that's where we focus most of our attention when we bring wealthy people together to have a conversation about money.

Us: Is there something special about bringing wealthy believers together?

TH: There sure is something special. The best way to encourage generosity is to tell stories and have a conversation. Biblically based teaching is wonderful and certainly is helpful, but the key ingredient is peers talking to peers about questions revolving around having a lot of money. It's a conversation about how to align our wealth and lifestyle with God's unique call on our lives. It's about experiencing the abundance that God wants for us. Wealth can be a source of great joy or a burden. God wants it to be a joy!

Us: What are some of the parts of these conversations that are unique for wealthy Christians?

TH: My wealthy Christian friends have special concerns and questions. Here are some of the thoughts and questions that come up when I talk with them:

- What about our kids? How do we enjoy our lifestyle without spoiling them?
- When we can afford just about anything, how do we decide what to buy?
- What are we losing in all this gaining?
- I know money doesn't equal happiness, but I thought I'd be a lot happier once I reached a certain level.
- Every time the pastor preaches on stewardship, I feel like he's got me in the crosshairs. Am I just paranoid?
- You probably think I'm crazy, but I actually worry about losing it all someday.
- I want to trust people, but I'm not sure who to trust.
- Sometimes I wonder if anyone likes me for who I am, or just for what I have.
- Is it possible to reclaim that innocence and freedom we experienced when we were just starting out and still have what we have?

Who can we talk to about the challenges and opportunities of wealth?

It's easy for the rest of us to think that if we had their wealth, life would be easy. But I do not recall any of my wealthy friends telling me that the larger their net worth, the easier it gets.

Us: You often refer to the interaction among wealthy Christians as a special conversation. What do you mean?

TH: The foundation for our conversation about generosity rests on the following six core principles from the Bible:

Principle #1
Giving Brings Joy

"Remembering the words the Lord Jesus himself said: 'It is more blessed to give than to receive" (Acts 20:35b).

I have seen this message validated over and over again in the lives of generous Christians. It is the "unexpected delight" that always results when someone decides to live generously. And while our focus is usually on money, this message also applies to giving our time or talent away.

Contrary to the message of popular culture that religion—specifically Christianity—takes all the fun out of life. Jesus offers a life that is not dependent upon wealth for happiness or pleasure. The truly abundant life that comes from obeying God has little to do with more stuff and everything to do with more freedom, peace, joy, adventure and purpose.

Principle #2
Giving Is a Heart Issue

"For where your treasure is, there your heart will be also" (Matthew 6:21).

I have been profoundly influenced by the writing of best-selling author Randy Alcorn. He advises, "If you want a heart for something, invest in it." And to illustrate he explains that if you invest in Google, you get more interested in news about Google. You follow it closely. There are lots of other tech companies, but you're more concerned about Google because you've invested in it.

Similarly, if you invest in the Kingdom of God, your heart grows for the things of the Kingdom. Giving generously leads to increased spiritual growth and vitality. You become the recipient of your own giving. This may be why the Bible has more to say about money than prayer or health.

Principle #3
God Gave First

"For God so loved the world that he gave his one and only Son" (John 3:16a).

God gave His Son, Jesus, who then gave His life for us. This is the ultimate example of generosity, and we are called to bear the image of God in all that we do. We, then, are most like God when we are generous.

Principle #4
Seek First God's Kingdom

"But seek first his kingdom and his righteousness, and all these things will be given to you as well" (Matthew 6:33).

What's most important to you? That's your priority. It can only be one thing. A priority is something that is more important to you than anything else and needs to be dealt with first. Most Christians would say that Jesus is more important to them than anything else. It's pretty easy to say, but in our conversations, we emphasize this message because so much is at stake. Earlier in Matthew, Jesus teaches that we can't serve both God and money, then adds this curious instruction: *"Therefore I tell you, do not worry about your life"* (Matthew 6:25a).

It's difficult to be generous if we worry about things, especially money. Conversely, if God and His ways are more important to us than anything else, we can be generous and not worry that we'll run out of "all these things." We have to be careful here. This is a promise about life, not about material wealth. Jesus is not telling us that if we give, we get more money in return. Rather, generosity produces the virtues of joy, peace, purpose and contentment that give life true meaning. At the same time, many of the people who have joined our conversation have significantly increased their generosity, yet I do not recall a single instance where anyone ran out of money because he or she gave too much away. But suppose someone did. Suppose he gave every penny away and his account hit zero. According to this promise, God will take care of him.

Principle #5
God Owns It All

"The earth is the Lord's, and everything in it" (Psalm 24:1a).

If you're a Christian, you've probably heard "God owns it all" hundreds of times, usually when the pastor preaches about stewardship. You may have even said it a few times yourself when a fellow believer alludes to your wealth: "Well, God owns it all. I'm just a steward." But what does that really mean?

It means when you are generous, you're really giving away someone else's money. That's what makes it fun. Truly generous people understand that they are God's money managers. Their wealth is not really theirs. Instead, they know that God has entrusted us with his resources so that we can use them as he directs. When we understand this biblical message, we become like that guy who hands out checks for the foundation. What a great job! I don't have to worry about sharing "my" money, because it really isn't mine. It all belongs to God.

Principle # 6
Heaven Is My Home

"But our citizenship is in heaven. And we eagerly await a Savior from there, the Lord Jesus Christ" (Philippians 3:20).

You've likely seen the illustration that Randy Alcorn and others have used to remind us our time on earth is brief, yet life in heaven continues forever. Draw a line across a piece of paper, then go back and make a dot with the tip of your pen or pencil just above the beginning of the line. The dot represents your time here on earth. Seventy, eighty, maybe ninety years. Seems like a long time, especially when you're in your thirties or forties. But compared to the line—eternity—it's barely a nanosecond. As Randy directs so succinctly and poignantly, "Live for the line, not for the dot."

Living for the line means that our primary focus is on what we can take with us, not on what will be left behind. All the money and the things that we buy stay. Who we truly are as children of God is all that we take with us so that we can enjoy a relationship with God forever. So why spend so much time on things that are temporary? Why not spend more time on drawing closer to God, becoming who he created and blessed with gifts and financial resources? Or to put it another way, if heaven is our true home, why worry about the furniture, appliances and landscaping that we can't take with us?

Generosity keeps us focused on what really matters, what really is important to God. When we are generous in Christ's name, we are furnishing our eternal home with treasures far greater than anything we can buy on earth. That doesn't mean spending money on nice things is wrong. It just might not be the best option, and certainly not the only option. Because in our heart's true home, none of that will matter.

Remember, the destination of the journey is not financial. We totally reject prosperity theology: name it and claim it, etc. The objective is not more money. The objective is for us to move ourselves and our loved ones closer to God. Money and giving is a challenging area where each yes toward generosity leads us closer to the heart of God. Paul warns us about the love of money causing all sorts of evil. Greed is like a disease. Generosity is the antidote.

Sidebar

Should believers give to secular organizations? The answer is: maybe. But if you do it should be largely separate from your

Kingdom giving. Howard Dayton, co-founder of Crown Financial Ministries, makes a great point in this regard. He says there are secular organizations and secular givers. There are Kingdom organizations and Kingdom givers. Kingdom givers might give to secular organizations, but secular givers never give to Kingdom organizations. Kingdom works need Kingdom givers!

Sidebar

In the conversation about generosity often the topic of street panhandlers often comes up; you know, the person on the street corner with a sympathy cardboard sign. I can't speak for everyone on this subject, and there are no "rules" per se. But my experience has been, and the advice of others with experience in this area is, don't give money. Ever. If you want to help, give food or personal hygiene items or a fast food gift card. Money will generally feed the problem that put them on the street corner to begin with. You might feel a temporary satisfaction as you drive away, but you likely just made their problem worse not better. It's far more helpful to give to the ministries who care for those people than to give them money directly. These ministries provide structure, accountability and process to the person's recovery and rehabilitation.

Janice

Janice Worth is on a mission to inspire other believers in their journey of generosity. She is generous, active, animated and impactful in her personal giving. Janice's wealth is self-made. She and her partner made their fortune via infomercials for their beauty care products in the 1980's. After coming to faith, Janice became an active supporter of ministries in New York and Palm Beach.

In addition to being involved in Generous Giving and the National Christian Foundation, Janice has been deeply impacted by the work of Women Doing Well. In the beginning, WDW conducted a survey of 7300 women of faith to assess their feelings, actions and attitudes about generosity. Based on those findings, they developed a one-day workshop as well as other resources to help women.

- To understand and focus on the purpose of their wealth
- To uncover their heart's passion for giving
- To develop a plan to act upon the purpose and passion

Janice reports that many women who have worked with WDW on their plans have a greater sense of clarity and enthusiasm for their giving, which has often led to giving increases of five times or more. Janice's giving passion is to help specific new ministries grow from early stage to viable ministry. She is a true venture philanthropist.

❓ *Points to Ponder*

1. Where are you on your generosity journey?

2. How can you prepare for the next phase of your journey?

3. What resources can you assemble to help with the journey?

4. How can you apply these best practices to move yourself along in your generosity journey?

➡ *Action Plan*

1. Attend a Generous Giving conference.

2. Schedule a lunch with a Christian foundation representative to see how they can help our family on our journey.

3. Take the NCF giving assessment.

Write your unique action items in the spaces provided below:

4. _____

_____

5. _____

_____

IMPACT

Chapter 5

Impact Givers Form a Team

"Plans fail for lack of counsel, but with many advisers they succeed" (Proverbs 15:22).

"Let the wise listen and add to their learning, and let the discerning get guidance" (Proverbs 1:5).

Impact giving should be a team effort. Giving as part of a team is more effective and more fun! By involving others, we have an opportunity for fellowship as we give. Generous giving builds generous relationships. Forming a team helps to overcome the isolation that wealthy Christians often feel. A well-rounded giving team should include the following:

1. **Spouse**

   It is disheartening to learn how many spouses feel excluded from the giving process in their family. Giving is a terrific experience to share, explore, bond, and grow with your spouse. (More on family giving in chapter 7.) Your spouse should be your partner in all giving decisions and plans. God has a purpose for including your spouse in your generosity opportunities, and you should intentionally explore that purpose together.

2. **Other family members (especially children and grandchildren)**

   One of the challenges for Christian families is to discover meaningful activities that can be shared by a group of people with ages ranging from newborn to 90s. It's not easy! Giving can cross over multiple generations and provide rich and meaningful shared experiences. (More on families in chapter 7.)

3. Generous peers

Something powerful happens when generous Christians get together. In our experience, there is no greater influence on a generous believer than a generous peer. There is instant credibility talking with someone who shares your experience, challenges and opportunities. Generous peers can fill a role that pastors and developmental people generally don't. Pastors and developmental people have rarely been asked for a large gift, and do not fully relate to the feelings involved. Generous peers offer a wealth of opportunities to learn, teach, share, collaborate, counsel and fellowship. Avoid stingy people. Stingy people will ruin your generosity journey. Stingy people will kill your generosity buzz. The biblical observation in Proverbs 27:17, "As iron sharpens iron so one person sharpens another," is especially true in the area of giving.

We have seen numerous examples where generous gifts were inspired on the spot by the actions of generous peers. Generosity is infectious. For our family our orphanage project was inspired in an instant. At an evening church service about 20 years ago, the pastor brought up for a testimony a local doctor who had just returned from building a medical clinic in Guatemala. As he told his story, Alex turned to his wife and said, "We could do that!" and she smiled and said "Maybe an orphanage?" And they did. That was all it took.

4. Mentor

Howard Hendricks has famously said, "Every man needs a Paul. Every man needs a Barnabas. Every man needs a Timothy." (To paraphrase for women: "Every woman needs a Paulette. Every woman needs a Barbara. Every woman needs a Tina.") A Paul/Paulette is a more mature believer to act as a mentor. A Barnabas/Barbara is an encouraging peer. A Timothy/Tina is a young person to pour into. It is a blessing to form these types of relationships. One thing we have learned over the years is that many successful people love the process of giving back. And while they often give money, they are often also willing to give back by sharing their wisdom and experiences with others. We both have had several mentors in our lives, and their presence has been a huge blessing in our marriages, parenting, careers and giving.

5. **Financial professionals (financial advisors, wealth managers, accountants and attorneys)**

If you want to excel in the gift of giving, you need to work with generous advisors! If you want your financial life to be built on solid biblical principles, you need to work with advisors who share your faith. It is a sad fact that most wealthy Christians do not work with advisors who share their faith. What a mistake! Technical competence is required of all advisors. That is a given. But how can an advisor who doesn't know God help you and your family move closer to Him? There is a difference between a financial professional who is a Christian and a Christian financial professional. Ideally, for your team to be effective, you should have advisors who can share wisdom and world view with your family.

It is imperative that you work with financial professionals who share your values and your passion for giving. If you don't, your best-laid plans won't be fully implemented. Too often, we've been "roadblocked" by CPAs and attorneys who don't understand what their client really wants.

Example:

We had a client who sold his business for about $15 million. He is very private person and has always done his giving under the radar. We suggested that he open up a donor-advised fund and gift shares of his company to the fund before the sale of the business so that he could avoid capital gains tax on that portion and still receive a charitable deduction. Everyone would win, except for Uncle Sam. But, his trusted CPA convinced him that he would be better off setting up a foundation after he sold the business.

This hurt the client in two ways:
1. He paid more in capital gains tax.
2. His giving was made public because he has a foundation. Just because it's a "private" foundation doesn't mean it's not available to the public. Every foundation in the United States files a form 990 and that information is made available on websites such as www.Guidestar.org.

When we showed my client that we could see who he gave to and how much was given, he was appalled.

Foundations are great. You just need to know if it's the right thing for you.

3. Foundation representatives

When you select your charitable institution for your giving fund, foundation, charitable trusts, etc., you can choose a secular organization or a faith-based organization. Which will help you advance in your faith walk of generosity? While there is nothing wrong with working with the major secular financial institutions, there are a large number of Christian foundations that can provide those same services as well as provide faith-based resources for your family. National Christian Foundation, Waterstone Foundation and Orchard Alliance Foundation are three of the foundations you might want to investigate. Most of these will allow you to continue to work with your current financial advisor and collaborate to make your giving plan happen.

4. National organizations

National organizations like Generous Giving, The Gathering and Women Doing Well are not-for-profit Christian organizations whose sole purpose is to provide resources to help your family grow in generosity.

5. Pastor

Your pastor may play an important role in helping you develop your gift for giving. Keep in mind that pastors' experience in this area varies greatly. Some pastors receive very little training in the gift of financial generosity. Some see their role as primarily about meeting their budget and capital needs. Others have a clear vision for discipling their people to be rich towards God. Have a conversation with your pastor and see if he might be a resource on your giving journey.

Sidebar

Impact givers often need to reprioritize the structure of their wealth management team. Traditional wealth management looks like this:

Secular Family Wealth Management Model

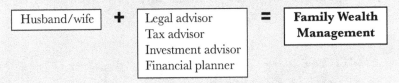

But a follower of Jesus Christ should have Him as the first priority in their wealth management:

Secular Family Wealth Management Plus Jesus Model

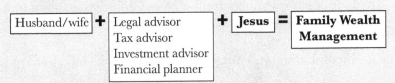

Faith-Based Family Wealth Management Model

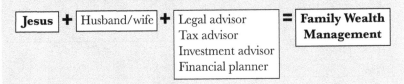

? Points to Ponder

1. How did you choose your professional advisors?

   Why did you choose them?

2. Do your advisors encourage your giving and help you advance on your generosity journey?

3. Are your closest peers generous?

4. Do your closest peers encourage your giving?

5. Who is on your giving team and why?

➡ Action Plan

1. Take my spouse to dinner to discuss forming our team.

2. Consider how our current advisors contribute to our generosity journey.

3. Identify some generous peers we would like to get to know better.

4. Identify a mentor.

Write your unique action items in the spaces provided below:

5. _____

   _____

6. _____

   _____

Chapter 6

Impact Givers Give More than Cash

[Content for this chapter is provided by Joseph Padilla, Vice President of The Orchard Alliance Foundation.]

Asset-based giving represents a huge opportunity for generous Christians to make their giving more effective. Christians in America hold 9% of their wealth in cash, yet 90% of giving is in the form of cash.

When Christians give to their church or other ministries they care about, most simply write a check. But, this is not always the best plan of stewardship.

Cash gifts are the most common type of giving, but there are other giving opportunities that allow us to make a greater Kingdom impact and receive more favorable tax benefits.

As stewards in God's Kingdom, we should take advantage of tax incentives available to us in order to harness as much as possible for the Lord's work and our families. So, if you're thinking of selling appreciated stock, appreciated real estate or a business, this is all a form of asset-based giving.

Often it is possible to receive greater tax benefits by giving assets such as:

- **Real Estate** – This includes residential as well as commercial property and land.
- **Life Insurance** – A charity can be named as owner or beneficiary or partial beneficiary of a life insurance policy.
- **IRA Funds** – Distributions from IRAs during one's lifetime as well as naming charities as beneficiaries of IRA accounts are often the most tax-efficient strategies. Charities

can also be named as beneficiaries of retirement accounts.

- **Public Stock** – Gift can reduce capital gains taxes.
- **Private Stock** – This can provide a way to transfer share ownership and create charitable deduction.
- **Proceeds** from the sale of a business.

Typically, when gifts of stock or real estate are made, any capital gains taxes on the asset are eliminated and a charitable income tax deduction can be created. These types of gifts typically require some planning ahead of time to ensure full tax benefits. This might include reduced or eliminated taxes if you include charitable giving as part of the strategy. With many types of non-cash gifts, the donor can opt to retain income from a gift transaction after it is completed.

Charitable Giving Vehicles to Consider

- **Donor-Advised Fund:** Allows donors to make tax-deductible gifts to the fund and to distribute the money to charity at a later date. This allows for more planning and control.
- **Private Foundation:** Similar to Donor-Advised Funds but is more sophisticated and generally requires larger amounts to establish, typically into the millions of dollars.
- **Charitable Trust:** Split-gift arrangement where the donor makes a gift today for a tax deduction but retains some rights to either income or principal from the gift.
- **Charitable Gift Annuity:** Is an exchange of an asset (usually appreciated in value) for a tax deduction and an income for life. The income payment is based on an age-based interest rate as set by the IRS.
- **Will Gifts:** Legacy gifts made via the last will and testament by individuals to Kingdom works that were important during their lifetime.

An effective asset-based giving strategy can release tax dollars you would ordinarily pay on the sale of the asset and instead pass those dollars to ministry. Those gifts could be more significant than you thought possible, multiplying your impact for God's Kingdom.

Asset-based giving has been around since biblical times. Consider how the Israelites sacrificially made non-cash gifts to build the Tabernacle (Exodus 25:1-9). They gave so much that Moses had to tell them to stop (Exodus 36:3-7). Do you remember how Barnabas and the others sold land and fields they owned and brought the money and laid it at the Apostles' feet (Acts 4:34-35)? Making non-cash gifts can be a great way to help accomplish your stewardship goals.

Tips on Asset-Based Giving

1. Look over your portfolio before making gifts to see if you have any appreciated assets to give instead of cash. Giving appreciated assets can yield larger tax benefits than giving cash.

   Mary and Don give their highest appreciated asset by percentage. (For example, if stock A is up 20% and stock B is up 25%, they give stock B.) Then, they use the cash they were going to give and repurchase the stock (assuming they still like the stock). They get their charitable deduction and increase their cost basis on the stock, so that if they sell it in the future (in lieu of giving it away), they'll pay less in capital gains tax.

2. Look for opportunities to give non-liquid assets like real estate, private company stock or other business interests.

3. Make sure your advisors are aware of your interest in giving appreciated assets and are competent to help you identify opportunities.

4. Retirement accounts can be very efficient sources of giving funds, both while you are alive and as part of your estate. Explore the best way to utilize IRAs 401ks, etc. as part of your family giving strategy.

   If you are over 70½, up to $100,000 of your annual required minimum distribution from IRAs may be distributed directly to a 501(c)(3) public charity, enabling you to avoid paying income taxes on that amount. This option is known as a qualified charitable distribution (QCD).

The QCD applies to traditional, rollover and Roth IRAs. SEP and Simple IRAs also qualify (as long as you are no longer actively receiving employer contributions). Employer-sponsored plans do not allow for QCD treatment.

5. Consider establishing a donor-advised fund or private foundation to help you manage the timing of your donating and distributions.

6. Add a relationship with a trusted foundation representative to your advisory team to get a new perspective on your giving plan.

Examples

1. Prior to selling his business, Mark placed a portion of the ownership in a private foundation. He received a tax deduction for the gift and avoided capital gains tax on that portion of the sale proceeds.

2. Every year end Matt and Sarah review their stock holdings to give their biggest winner to their favorite ministry. This gives them a tax deduction as well as avoids capital gains taxes.

3. Sam and Amy use a donor-advised fund for most of their giving. This fund allows them to make their gifts when funds are available, but distribute to ministries at a later date if that fits their giving plan.

4. Wilma gave a piece of land to her favorite ministry in a charitable gift annuity arrangement that enabled her to avoid capital gains tax, receive a charitable deduction and Wilma will receive an income for the rest of her life.

5. Clint loved his local church. In his will left his estate in equal portions to his three beloveds: two children and his church!

❓ *Points to Ponder*

1. What assets can you give that are more effective than giving cash?

2. How can you work with your advisors to incorporate asset-based giving into your financial planning and giving strategies?

3. How can Christian foundations and ministry development representatives help you give assets instead of cash?

4. How can asset-based giving increase your giving capacity?

5. How can a donor-advised fund or private foundation fit into your giving plan?

6. Can you find ways to save even more taxes when you give?

➡ *Action Plan*

1. Consult with our financial advisor about opportunities for asset-based giving.

2. Meet with representatives from Christian foundations to discuss how we can give more effectively.

IMPACT

Write your unique action items in the spaces provided below:

3. _____

_____

4. _____

_____

5. _____

_____

Chapter 7

Impact Givers Involve Their Family

Family giving represents one of the greatest benefits in the giving journey.

Family giving reaches across generations. Family giving allows parents, grandparents and others to connect, bond and influence the next generations. When families give of their time, talent and treasure together, God often shows up in special ways and blesses families and relationships.

Family giving transfers values in a tangible way. There is no more powerful way to lead children and grandchildren than by modeling generous behavior. Watching Grandpa or Mom act as the hands and feet of Jesus can leave an unforgettable, life-changing vision in the hearts of other family members.

Family giving is a bonding experience among family members. Bonding experiences are formed by effort and priority. Family members love to be part of "what we do" as a family. Family generosity creates family culture and family identity. Mission trips, sharing, feeding the homeless all become part of a shared identity that makes us who we are as a family.

Family giving provides a Christ-centered reason to keep in touch. As families grow and get older and move, common ground can start to disappear. Giving together can be one of the ties that bind.

Family giving is fun. Why not share with those you love most your most satisfying experiences?

Family giving allows older generations to mentor and act as role models. Younger generations are going to believe something and look up to someone. It might as well be you!

The most powerful, important, impactful giving we have witnessed is when the vision and resources of a ministry and the vision of a motivated, generous Christian family come together.

The following short story by Abby illustrates our potential generosity purpose in our intended vocation. While she chooses a seemingly glamorous career, her motive and purpose for the career may surprise and inspire most of us.

"Abby, Abby! Come over here! I need you for my new movie," said my producer, Mr. Quacky. I love being a move star because of my fame, the fantastic movies that I'm in and the money I earn.

For starters, the best part of being a movie star is all the fame. The fame makes me popular. All the popularity is one thing that made me become a movie star. There is one exhausting moment about my job and being popular—all the paparazzi.

"Oh please, STOP! The camera flashes are blinding me!"

The thing about fame could be amazing too. That part is...LIMOS! As I get in the black shiny limo, I stare at all of the soda, which I'm used do. Then my driver drives me to my new movie premiere. I get out of my limo and walk on the red carpet. Fame is the way.

As a movie star learning all the lines for the new movie "Dance" (which is coming out summer 2020) was probably the hardest movie to learn. The best part and the main things of a movie star is to learn your lines. What I do is I go through my script. I find all my lines and highlight them. Then I memorize. Another thing is when you are a movie star like me you get to always be the star of the movie.

In my new movie "Dance" the main role is Rebecca or Bekie. I was chosen. The star always has the most lines. You don't ever miss your chance to be in a movie.

Money is another part of being a movie star. Number one,

giving away my money really puts a smile on my face. I like to give my money away to the needy. It really helps them because of all the money I make. After a whole week of giving the money to the Browns, they weren't needy anymore.

I can also keep some money to myself. Did you know that I only keep a quarter of my money? Instead of making millions, I make ten thousands, hundred thousands. You may think that "Oh, the best part of being a movie star is to keep all the money." But NO! It's about giving it to people who really need it.

A movie star can be a lot of work. All the fame and movies. Like I said before, making millions of dollars is not just the best part. The best part is to give your money away to the people who really need it.

As Randy Alcorn wisely points out, generosity is the antidote for materialism. Unchecked, materialism can grow into a condition called "affluenza": a psychological malaise affecting wealthy young people. Growing up in an unhealthy wealth-oriented environment can lead to lack of motoviation, feelings of guilt, emptiness and isolation. Symptoms include anxiety, compulsive spending, gambling, debt and a general sense of lack of well-being disconnected from life circumstances. Did you ever think your wealty could cause a psychological malaise in your children? Generosity can help innoculate against affluenza!

Seeds (Dave's story)

Dave has often been asked how he became so passionate about orphans; what led him to do international adoptions and start an orphange. Dave's response was that it had just always been part of him. One day his friend said, "Well, it came from somewhere. What is your earliest memory of caring about orphans?" And bingo, it was as clear as if it happened yesterday.

Dave was in second grade. It was 1964. Back then the mail

came twice a day and he went to school half days because there were too many kids for the available classrooms (milk was delivered to his steps every morning by the milk man). He was in the middle of his four-year streak of nothing but bologna sandwich lunches. His mom was opening the morning mail, and in it Dave saw a picture of a little Asian girl. He asked about it and his mom said, "Her name is Mae Ling, she lives on Formosa and we sponsor her."

"What is sponsor?" he asked.

"We send her $10 a month."

"Why would we do that?"

"Because her family is poor and can't take care of her."

Dave's mom's words hit him like a lighting bolt. He looked down at his bologna sandwich (in triangles with the crust cut off and the glass of milk just delivered to his front stoop) and the idea that every kid in the world didn't have those basic needs stunned him and broke his heart. He couldn't believe that there were kids who didn't have all their needs taken care of. It riveted him! As Bob Pierce of World Vision famously said, "Let my heart be broken by things that break the heart of God."

Years passed. Dave grew up and got a job. The first thing he did with extra money was sponsor a child. Then a few more, then a few more. He got up to 30 sponsored children. Dave got married, had a son. Then unexplained infertility for 10 years. During that time they adopted two girls; one from Korea and one from China. Dave and his wife partnered with others to build an orphanage in Central America. They adopted from that orphanage too. Their giving passion for the fatherless and orphaned grew and grew. It is core to their faith walk and their family identity.

Dave is thankful that he had a godly mom who was such a great model of generosity and planted the seeds in his heart. He is also thankful for that picture of Mae Ling, how it touched his heart so long ago and set the passion compass of his life in a plan that only God can author. He marvels at how much the picture of Mae Ling looks like their two Asian daughters.

Some of the ways to facilitate family involvement are:

Vision trips: When we talk to wealthy Christian families, the number one, most impactful act they describe in helping foster family generosity is mission trips. Getting out of the First World and into impoverished areas, even within the U.S., is an eye-opening and heart-changing experience. Families will become more sensitive to the needs of the least of these when they have actually seen the needs up close and personal. Connecting with the poor is a door opener. Henry Blackaby has said that in God's economy, the rich and the poor need each other. The poor need the rich to meet their physical needs, and the rich need the poor to help meet their spiritual needs. Something to think about.

Ministry visits: A family visit to the local crisis pregnancy center, after school program or soup kitchen puts names and flesh to the concept of compassion and mercy like no book or sermon can. The essence of the Gospel can be best experienced by experience. St. Francis of Assisi said, "Preach the Gospel at every opportunity. Use words if necessary."

Conferences: Including your family members at conferences can help tap into a wealth of resources and networks for the giving journey. Organizations like Generous Giving, the Gathering and Women Doing Well offer excellent content in a non-selling not-for-profit environment to help attendees grow in their generosity journey. They are excellent environments for networking with other like-minded individuals and families who have had the same experiences and challenges as you.

Matching gifts: Contributing alongside family members to causes important to them can be an experience of encouragement and unity. It is a great opportunity to support and encourage your family members to begin to form their own generosity vision and create the means to support it. Like all the other areas of personal finance, giving must be taught. Giving is most effectively reproduced when it is modeled. Matching gifts allow you to show family members how to have "skin in the game."

Holiday events: The holiday season is the easiest time to get family members to think about giving. There is something about the season that gets the generosity juices flowing. Charities report that over 30% of their donations comes during the end of the holiday season. You can easily use the season of generosity to encourage participation by your family. This season especially appeals to your kids, but it can be an entry point for older people to a generosity journey. It is critically important that we remember that generosity is a 365-a-year activity. But the holiday season is a great time to focus your family members.

Decision-making: Make the family giving budget a family decision. Share the decision-making process and giving decisions with family members. Let them experience ownership. Show them what you have learned about the process of working with ministries and churches as an engaged impact donor. Fill in the details. Show them how to roll up their sleeves and dig in to the giving process, including the following decisions:

- Who do you give to?
- How to form a strategic vision?
- How much to give?
- How often to give?
- What assets to give?
- How to evaluate the work that was funded?
- When to stop giving?

Construction projects: There is profound power in investing in manual labor, building houses, schools, churches, etc. Construction is especially rewarding because there is a tangible result at the end. We don't always know if prayers are answered or counsel accepted, but we know when the building is done!

Volunteering: Share the experience, build a house, feed the homeless, tutor a child, help a teen mom care for a baby, get to know ministries, their people and their work—together.

Giving fund: Give family members a giving fund and meet regularly to discuss what they have given and why. Give together!

"Paid" intern: Pay your kids a normal part-time job wage to volunteer longer term at a ministry. Danny told his kids they could better serve the Kingdom as "paid interns," more so than working at Subway or the local supermarket. They all made valuable contributions to the ministries and churches where they worked, got great experience, and these led directly to their first paying jobs. Danny had this arrangement with his three oldest children and the experience for them was priceless.

Needs close to home: It is a great real-world experience as a family to identify needs in the community around them and help make a difference. We all know people with needs. By being open-minded, watchful and Spirit-led, family members may see the need to pray for and help another family right in their own school, church or community.

Family projects: Select a specific project to take on as a family, something you can all be part of and do together.

Danny's family

Danny's family became involved in an orphanage in Central America. Their initial gift to build the facility has led to a 15-year relationship. Two of their daughters were adopted from the orphanage. Their five other children went on over 50 mission trips to visit the kids. It became an integral part of their growing up years.

Impact? Danny's son was fourteen years old when they visited the orphanage for the first time. After three days with the kids they were sitting on the runway waiting to take off for their return flight home.

"Dad, you know the family trip to Disney next month?" he asked.

"Yes." Danny replied.

"Is it already paid for?"

"Yes, why?"

"Any chance we can get the money back and come here instead?"

WOW.

Danny's oldest daughter is **Sasha**. She is a wonderful blessing, a truly godly young woman whom he was blessed to adopt from Korea as a baby. She made her first mission trip when she was six years old. One day they were at the beach town of La Libertad, El Salvador. The sun was setting over the Pacific as they encountered three teenage local girls who were selling plastic jewelry to make a living. They spent about $40 on about $4 worth of jewelry and then hopped in the car to go back to their hotel. When Danny sat down, he felt a bottle of water on his seat. Without really giving it a thought, he flipped the bottle out to the three girls. They looked at the bottled water in total fascination! They passed it back and forth and held it up to the sunlight. After a very animated conversation in Spanish, they unscrewed the cap and passed the bottle one to another, each taking one mouthful only at a time until it was all gone.

It occurred to him that bottled water is a luxury to them. As tears filled his eyes, he felt Sasha's breath on his neck from the back seat, leaning forward close to his ear and saying, "I love you, Daddy!"

Upon their return to their hotel room, they had a quick devotion before dinner. They were working their way through Matthew one verse at a time, and Danny turned to the verse of the day, Matthew 10:42, "And if anyone gives even a cup of cold water to one of these little ones…that person will certainly not lose their reward." Do you think that made an impression on her?

Twelve years later, Sasha had her first car. One day Danny noticed a lot of junk in her back seat. Playing the dad card he asked her, "Why the mess? " It's not a mess," she explained. She took him to her car and showed him what he thought was junk was in fact piles of zip lock baggies filled with socks, deodorant and other personal items. "I don't want to give the homeless people money, but I want to help them, so I give them these and water bottles."

Ann is a very low-key mom from a very wealthy family. She and her husband have worked for years during summer break serving the poor in Appalachia. This year they brought their 12-year-old son, Spencer. He immediately connected with a local 12-year-old named Tim. For a week they were inseparable, building walls, picking up garbage and other chores. At the end of the week the team decided to bless Tim with a $20 Walmart gift card. Spencer had the privilege of giving Tim the gift. He blessed his new friend and returned very quietly to his parent's car. "What's up?" they asked. "Did you give Tim the card?"

"Yes."

"What did he say?"

"Thank you."

"Did you ask him what he is going to do with the money?"

Spencer was quiet for a moment and then with a crackly voice said, "Deodorant. He said he has always wanted to have deodorant. He has never had it before and wants to make sure he smells good when he goes to school."

These experiences definitely leave a mark!

Here are some tips on how you can include your family:

1. If you are married, include your spouse: he or she is your partner, and doing your giving as partners is great for your marriage.
2. Lead by example: children consider what they hear but model what they see.
3. Be intentional: make including your family a priority until it becomes part of the family culture.
4. Examine how your family spends its time and see if adjustments can be made to be more God honoring.
5. Have a family conversation and include everyone in the process.

Final point: History is full of stories of the rise and fall of wealthy families. Family money has a spiritual power and influence. In your family, will that power be good or bad?

The Family Conversation Guide

[Used with permission from David Wells,
President Emeritus, National Christian Foundation]

The following four steps below will give you an outline to follow as you prepare and pursue this collective goal of forming a Family Stewardship Philosophy. Remember, the purpose of this initiative is to encourage your family toward realizing God's calling for your stewardship together.

Developing and stating your philosophy togeter provides several benefits:

STRENGTHEN: your convictions about the purpose of wealth and its most appropriate uses.

PROMPT: family members to reflect on personal beliefs about the source of possessions.

IDENTIFY: the values at stake when wealth is transferred, and develop a practical plan for estate distribution to children, heirs and other beneficiaries.

CLARIFY: purposeful intentions behind inheritance plans, and recognize opportunities to develop preparedness among beneficiaries.

Step One - Engage

Every family has its own unique persona and circumstances. The idea of approaching family members to talk about estate matters is either appealing, intimidating or somewhere in-between.

Trust your instincts. Your intuition is a helpful guide when deciding how and when to introduce this process. You must also decide whom to include. Ideally, all adult children—and probably their spouses—are relevant to the discussion. Just recognize that it might not be possible to avoid awkwardness and discomfort completely. But in the end, the permanent rewards of this family experience far outweigh the temporary feelings you may need to endure along the way. Find whatever courage you need to keep your family from being deprived of these blessings. However you personalize it, the first step is to introduce each person to the concept of a Family Stewardship Philosophy. Tell them how this idea came to your attention, and why it has meaning for you. Let them know your vision of what to expect from the process—what commitments are required and what benefits will result. If appropriate, give them some time to absorb the idea and let them know you'll be following up in the near future.

Step Two - Prepare

As the parent, it's important for you to have a solid command of your convictions, values and objectives related to your estate. You are the leader. And while you don't have to be overpowering, your preparedness will set the tone for other family members. The more they sense that you take it seriously, the more they will be encouraged to do the same. It is recommended that you personally think through each of the components of the Family Stewardship Philosophy on your own before meeting with others. When you know where you stand, you will be free to listen and encourage others to explore an express their feelings, desires and priorities.

Step Three - Gather

Whether you convene once, or interact over several meetings, the family gathering is essential to the process. Your family's situation may dictate the logistics. But getting together enables open discussion and the most efficient communication. The format of your time(s) together depends on personal factors; however, the goals before you are the same. Each person should be asked to comment on the components of the Family Stewardship Philosophy. You may want to address them in order:

Begin with a brief overview of your life (lives) and those things that have impacted your beliefs.

Develop a Statement of Purpose

- What is your family's collective purpose?
- With regard to wealth management, what role does the family play in God's universe?

Express Convictions about the Source of Wealth

- If God owns it all, what does it mean that He has entrusted the family with possessions?

Take Inventory of Motives Surrounding Wealth

- Why accumulate wealth? What temptations exist that might have negative consequences?

Examine the Value of Goals

- What is the purpose of lifetime preservation of the family estate?
- What is the purpose of lifetime distribution?

Define a Philosophy for Utilization

- What lifestyle is reasonable?
- How will you define and regulate personal lifestyle goals to protect against materialism?
- What is your "financial finish line"?

Decide on a plan for Wealth Transition

- Are there any unspoken expectations regarding an inheritance?
- What do the family's stewardship goals suggest about the balance of giving before death and inheritance?
- What do the family objectives suggest about the timing of wealth transfer?

Family Study Questions: The following study questions can also be helpful to facilitate discussion:

ACQUISITION

Read: Deuteronomy 8:11, 14, 18

"Be careful that you do not forget the LORD your God, failing to observe his commands, his laws and his decrees that I am giving you this day....Then your heart will become proud and you will forget the LORD your God, who brought you out of Egypt, out of the land of slavery....But remember the LORD your God, for it is he who gives you the ability to produce wealth, and so confirms his covenant, which he swore to your ancestors, as it is today."

1. To what factors do you attribute the acquisition of your wealth?
2. What purpose do you see in the ownership/use of wealth? (i.e., What motivates you to acquire it?)
3. What influences have shaped your thinking about money, its acquisition and use? What passages of Scripture, collateral writings, experiences or individuals have been most meaningful to you in this regard? What do they teach you?
4. Assuming you will continue to acquire assets, what will characterize such acquisition? What will your family, busi-

ness partners and employees think about you as you continue to accumulate wealth?

5. How would you explain the common and primary values (spiritual, financial, etc.) shared by the members of your family?

6. Where on your list of priorities does the acquisition of wealth fall?

PRESERVATION

Read: Proverbs 30:7-9

"Two things I ask of you, LORD; do not refuse me before I die: Keep falsehood and lies far from me; give me neither poverty nor riches, but give me only my daily bread. Otherwise, I may have too much and disown you and say, 'Who is the LORD?' Or I may become poor and steal, and so dishonor the name of my God."

1. Why have you preserved some of your wealth?

2. What are the reasons for preserving your wealth as opposed to giving it away?

3. How do you balance preservation and faith?

4. What Scripture or principles guide you in determining how you are to preserve your wealth? (such as saving or giving away)

5. Have you set a goal as to what amount, or percentage, of your wealth you will preserve?

SPENDING

Read: 1 Timothy 6:17-18

"Command those who are rich in this present world not to be arrogant nor to put their hope in wealth, which is so uncertain, but to put their hope in God, who richly provides us with everything for our enjoyment. Command them to do good, to be rich in good deeds, and to be generous and willing to share."

1. Do you feel that the spending of your wealth brings with it responsibilities or obligations?

2. What are the primary alternatives you have with regard to spending wealth?

FAMILY

1. How do you react to the idea of a family foundation or an NCF Giving Fund that is used by the family as a vehicle from which gifts are made?
2. How, if at all, do you see financial gifts as a tool for instilling character, responsibility, spiritual maturity, etc. in your children and others?
3. If you regularly give to your children, why do you do so? If you do not, why not?
4. Ideally, what type of family involvement in the gift decision process would seem to be most fulfilling for your family during your life?

CHARITABLE GIVING

1. Concerning charitable giving, what compels you to give?
2. To what extent is your charitable giving each year driven by your income tax status?
3. Have you developed a list of criteria or a mission statement that guides your giving? If yes, please delineate.
4. How do you evaluate the impact of your gifts and/or hold your specific charities accountable?
5. Where are your passions and priorities when it comes to charitable giving?
6. What is your perspective on tithing?
7. What priority does giving hold in the list of ways you utilize your wealth?

TRANSITION

Read: Luke 12:20

"But God said to him, 'You fool! This very night your life will be demanded from you. Then who will get what you have prepared for yourself?'"

1. What is your primary goal in transferring your wealth?
2. How does that goal serve God's Kingdom?
3. Does your plan take the latest tax laws into account?
4. What legal instruments need to be in place to achieve your wealth transfer goals?

5. How should you communicate with the recipients of your estate in order to prepare?
6. How frequently will you update your plan?

Step Four - Document

One of the most important steps is to write a draft of your responses to step three above. By documenting your family's discussion and ideas, you create a tangible reference point that can be shared among family members. This will reinforce your convictions and encourage unity. It also makes it easier to recall the conversations and revise your thoughts as they develop.

Consider this:

Why will your children's children share your Family Stewardship Philosophy?

If you have children, you know every family has an ever-changing nature about it. Not long after children arrive in our homes, they become adults more quickly than we could ever imagine. Most of them become parents and experience the dizzying fast-forward world of parenting for themselves. Sometimes it seems there isn't enough time to prepare our children for adulthood. They're out the door before we've had a chance to give them all they need.

What growing, changing, evolving families need are foundations. Not just moral and spiritual foundations, but firm foundations that anchor them financially. That's why developing a Family Stewardship Philosophy is so important. It lays the groundwork for all your decisions about wealth. While it's possible to pass on monetary wealth to your family, it's even more essential to pass on a philosophy. The questions posed through this section are not designed just to make you think. They are meant to lead to answers that are solid enough to remain relevant for generations to come.

For further information visit: www.ncfgiving.org

? *Points to Ponder*

1. What opportunities do you have to increase your family's involvement in your giving?

2. Where can your family volunteer together in your local community?

3. Is your family ready for a vision trip?

4. Can your family attend a generosity conference in the year ahead?

5. Do your family members articulate a shared generosity philosophy?

▶ *Action Plan*

1. Create a family giving statement as a family.

2. Plan a family vision trip.

3. Ask family members where they would like to give this year.

Write your unique action items in the spaces provided below:

4. _____

    _____

5. _____

    _____

Chapter 8

Success vs. Significance

"Do not store up for yourselves treasures on earth, where moths and vermin destroy, and where thieves break in and steal. But store up for yourselves treasures in heaven, where moths and vermin do not destroy, and where thieves do not break in and steal. For where your treasure is, there your heart will be also" (Matthew 6:19-21).

Impact Givers understand there is a huge difference between "success" and significance. Worldly success can be fleeting, shallow and empty. Solomon, in Ecclesiastes 4:4, called earthy success, "Vanity, like chasing after the wind." Thousands of years later, those words are still true as we witness countless celebrities, who enjoy all that life on earth can offer, fall into ruin. Significance is different. Significance reaches outside of our own life and into the lives of others. Significance reaches outside of our time and connects our efforts to eternity. Eternal significance starts when we start asking, "What can I do today for God?" Significance lasts.

Martin Luther observed, "I have held many things in my hands and I have lost them all. But whatever I have placed in God's hands I still possess."

The quest for significance keeps us young and sharp. Our culture tells us that we should use the first half of our lives to provide for our financial needs, and the second half of life is about leisure, travel, golf, etc. Is there something more? Think about it. By the time we reach our 50s and 60s, we are at our peak in terms of wisdom, knowledge, experience and financial, social and relational capital. Do we just squander all that for the sake of leisure? Peter Drucker has famously said, "We overprepare for the first half of life and underprepare for the second half."

Impact Givers recognize that the work they did in the first half of life is a God-given opportunity and serves as a platform for great Kingdom works in the second half of life. The same gifts and talents that have allowed wealth and personal financial security to be accumulated can be redirected towards countless causes, ministries and Kingdom passions in a new and impactful way. Remember, none of the heroes in the Bible ever retired! Significance keeps us engaged, involved, relevant and sprinting towards the finish line!

Special Guest

The Season of Halftime
By Paul McGinnis, Halftime Institute

Just a little over a hundred years ago the average life span of the American male was around 50 years, with women living a little longer than that. Work for most people was arduous and taxing and life was, for the most part, much harder than it is today. Survival was the goal, and thriving or finding one's passion was far down on most people's to-do list.

Today, when we reach 50, most of us have 25-30 good years left. We are experienced and we have built a lifetime of relationships and trust. Combine all of that with the fact that we are probably better off financially and have more time than we had in our younger years, and it's easy to see why the question of "what's next for me?" would come up.

In a way, it's a perfect storm. Suddenly we are offered the privilege of taking our unique set of skills, talents, passions and relationships and using them in a different way, if not in a different setting altogether.

Bob Buford began a movement more than two decades ago, one that offered answers to the growing throng of people who have experienced success in "Life I" and want to be sure that they finish well in "Life II." After going through halftime himself, Bob found that he was overprepared for Life I and wholly underprepared for Life II, and that there was no university for one's second half.

He set about to change that. His groundbreaking book, *Halftime: Moving from Success to Significance* found a wide audience and has been read by millions since it was first published in 1995. "At best I thought I'd sell a few thousand copies and that would be it," he says. Instead he tapped into an emerging trend that continues today, unabated.

After the success of *Halftime*, Buford continued to research and write on the subject. He launched the Halftime Institute, the University for Your Second Half, an organization whose alumni have gone on to do remarkable things around the world.

"Smoldering Discontent"

The system we live and work in every day is set up to encourage us to keep moving forward without a lot of introspection, isn't it? We sort of revere those who have "made it" and are living in the big house and driving the newest cars. Business schools teach us how to make more and what they tell us creates a paragon of success that we begin to chase but never catch. The billionaire John Rockefeller was supposedly asked, "How much is enough?" His reply, "Just a little bit more." That philosophy is still deeply ingrained in our culture.

And so, armed with all of our good intentions and a little knowledge, we head out into the business world and begin to make money for ourselves and others. We even choose careers, not based on what we dream about or what our gifts and talents may be, but which pursuit pays the most.

On top of that, we are encouraged by those we are making money for to focus on making even more. Corporations report on their earnings quarterly, and the numbers have to keep going up and up or we lose our jobs, no matter the high price we are paying elsewhere in our marriages, with our children or our friends. Forward and upward is all that matters.

But then, one day it happens for some of us. We've amassed

wealth, bought all the toys we could buy, and we are sitting in our corner office thinking how great we must be to have been so successful. We longed for it and we got it. But then, the smoldering discontent begins, that feeling that this can't be all I was expected to do with this one life of mine, these 70 or 80 years on this planet. Surely there is more.

This unease that we feel that drives us to look for answers is accompanied by other leading indicators that one is in the season of halftime:

- Sensing a transition or refocus of some kind
- Desire for more joy, peace, fulfillment
- Passion to make a difference
- Desire for more balance regarding work, family and other commitments

There are three key answers that each individual who is in the season of halftime must solve for in order to navigate this journey in a healthy way:

CORE

"What is your passion? What have you achieved? What have you done uncommonly well? How are you wired? Where do you belong? What are the "shoulds" that have trailed you during the first half? These and other questions like them will direct you toward the self your heart longs for; they will help you discover the task for which you were especially made."

—Bob Buford

Your Core is made up of three main elements: Passions, Strengths and a Mission Statement. Passions are the issues and causes that keep you energized. The things that fire you up and get you out of bed in the morning. The Christian philosopher Soren Kierkegaard said, in so many words, that the key to life is to find the cause you'd be willing to live or die for. That's what we mean by passions.

Another part of your Core is Strengths. Strengths are the things that come natural to you and those areas you've gotten good at over the years through training or experience. It also includes your spiritual gifts and skills and aptitudes that are innate... just a part of your God-given DNA. Finding creative ways to use your strengths in your areas of passion can make a big difference in peoples' lives and bring you great joy and fulfillment.

The final aspect of Core is your Mission Statement. This is not just your dream for yourself. A mission statement converges your strengths, passions and desired outcomes into a sentence that defines who you are, what you desire to serve, and what you intend to do with your life. It enables you to stay focused on what you believe God has called you to do. Crafting a mission statement is NOT an attempt to design your life or future, but in contrast, it's about listening carefully for God's unique assignment and having the courage to put it down in writing. It will help you stay the course of God's agenda for your life within the context of His greater plan for the world.

CAPACITY

"Desire alone will not allow you to do something new in your second half. You must create the capacity to do it. If you are being controlled by too many time- and energy-consuming activities, you will continue to be frustrated by unfulfilled dreams and desires."

—Bob Buford

The second big issue you must solve for is Capacity—having the capacity to live out our mission. If we spend all of our time, money and energy on ourselves and our families, we have nothing left to offer others.

There are three components to address in the area of Capacity. The first is Time: You need to have, or be willing to create, margin in your calendar in order to discover and pursue your calling. If you have no time to think and act outside of your current day-to-day obligations, you'll never be able to make the changes you want.

The next Capacity area to address relates to the degree that we have, or can create, financial margin. Having financial margin frees us up to give ourselves to a cause or purpose that's greater than ourselves. I'm not talking about the idea that you need to be a financially independent philanthropist before you can pursue significance. That's a myth of Halftime. Halftime is more about availability than affluence. As part of solving for this big issue, you and your spouse will need to answer the question "How much is enough?"

The last piece of Capacity is Spiritual Overflow. We create spiritual capacity to live out our mission by keeping our spiritual tanks filled to overflowing. A life of significance is, by Jesus' definition, a life of sacrifice—loving God and others so much that we are willing to give ourselves away to meet peoples' deepest needs. We can't love others in a sustainable way, even when it's in the zone of our strengths and passions, if we aren't overflowing with God's love. Your coach will help you build a spiritual development strategy that suits your personality, learning style and spiritual maturity.

CONTEXT

"Align yourself with islands of health and strength. Work with those who want to work with you."

—Peter Drucker

The third "C" is Context. In parallel to getting clear on your Core and creating Capacity, you can begin the creative process of designing the Context that will allow you to live out your calling.

There are two pieces to Context—the first is your Role. Most ministry happens in the context of a team, rather than in isolation. Knowing what role or roles you play best on a team enables you to serve in the most effective manner. Rather than default to a board member role or an operational staff role, you may need to broaden your vision and creativity.

If you were a consultant or entrepreneur in your first half, you may discover that your first half role is your best contribution in the second half as well. It may be that a lot of what you did in your first half was training for your second. Alternatively, many executives, entrepreneurs and professionals are living joyful, world-changing second halves doing something completely different from their first half career. With a little thought you can define the role(s) you enjoy that will allow you to make the greatest contribution in a sustainable way.

The other piece of Context is the organization in which you'll serve. Let's be clear—this is less about a "for profit v. nonprofit" decision and more about using your gifts in a way that brings you joy and makes a difference in peoples' lives. There are three options as it relates to Context. The first is to stay exactly where you are. For many Halftimers, their current marketplace position provides the perfect platform for them to live out their calling. By tweaking your activities and time allocation, you may begin to see the impact you long for, right where you are. Sometimes we jump to the conclusion that Halftime is about selling your company and going to seminary or bailing from your job and moving to Africa. The fact is, a large percentage of Halftimers end up finding creative ways to more joy and impact right where they are and never leave their current workplace. In those cases, it's not about doing something different. It's about doing things differently.

The second option is to join an organization, or perhaps several organizations, already working on an issue you have a passion for. No need to reinvent the wheel if there is "an island of health and strength" that already has momentum and credibility working on an issue you care about.

The third option is to start your own organization or ministry. Some of you are entrepreneurs and have the ability to see opportunities and create organizations. You may not be well suited to working within an established organization.

Don't feel compelled to have the answers to your Context challenge figured out right now. It takes time. Designing your second half context often requires testing out several options. Don't be discouraged if you try three or four things before you find the right fit.

The mission of the Halftime Institute is to come alongside people in this season of halftime and coach them into a productive and fulfilling second half. And, make no mistake about it: coaching is critical to the process. As Margie Blanchard has well said, "It's the program that gets you started, but it's the coaching that makes it happen."

The Halftime Fellows Program

The Halftime Institute's highly successful Fellows Program features a blend of faith and leading-edge instruction; personal time with thought leaders and top authors; one-on-one executive guidance, and peer exchange at the highest levels.

The program also includes:

Peer collaboration. Halftime Fellows are elite marketplace achievers poised to know and pursue God's call for their second half of life. Given their love of Christ and a common desire for significance and surrender, peer relationships are one of the program's chief benefits.

"Head" and "heart" curricula. Each Fellow will design a personal spiritual growth plan, a mission statement and an action plan—this is the Heart Journey. The Head Journey, guides Fellows through concepts, readings, speakers, discussions, coaching and best practices. The paths come together in exposure to thought leaders and practitioners of leading-edge and global work in education, poverty, microfinance, orphan and widow care, healthcare and medicine, food and clean water, and social justice.

Leading thinkers and practitioners. Jim Collins, Bob Buford, Ken Blanchard and Margie Blanchard and similarly renowned thinkers, speakers and influencers bring both news-making insights and rare personal interaction. As do leaders in faith-based organizations from all over the world such as Rich Stearns, Chris Crane, Peter Greer and many others.

Coaching by a Halftime Institute Certified Coach. Each Fellow has both regular meetings and 24/7 access to our best, most seasoned Halftime coaches—a personal, one-on-one "head and heart" guide through the full year.

Personalized & Exclusive Events. The Halftime Fellows year is a sequence of intimate group meetings, events, and discussions; one-on-one coaching; a couple's retreat; specialized webinars and teleconferences; readings and interaction with leading speakers and authors; and, as your ideas and decisions take shape, introductions and hands-on experience to help you explore your areas of interest.

Testimony
A Success to Significance Story: Scott Boyer

Scott Boyer spent 27 years working in the pharmaceutical business and was familiar with the sales of products in all areas of the world.

It was during this time that he realized that the wealthiest countries had the most significant sales, but the "rest of the world," the ROW countries where the majority of the people live, didn't have access to life-changing medications or treatment. Scott started to dream about how he could help these ROW countries but faced pushback and discouragement from those around him.

At this strategic time, a new friend came into Scott's life and encouraged him to read the book Halftime.

"I read it soon after he gave it to me" Scott said. "The book helped to see there were many others like me that God was calling to a second half of significance, but most were not sure how to proceed. I called the Halftime Institute to explore next steps and before I knew it, I was attending the April 2014 Launch Event surrounded by like-minded peers."

Scott had clarity of vision but needed the encouragement and guidance that a coach could bring. He joined the Halftime Fellows Program and worked through the year with his coach, zeroing in on and refining what would be next for him.

Scott is now the founder and president of The ROW Foundation and OWP Pharmaceutical. OWP and ROW are already having an impact in parts of the world that, up to now, did not have access to much-needed epilepsy drugs. Their impact is already being felt in such far-flung places as Armenia and Haiti and beyond.

So, what will you do with your 30 or so extra years? More and more that is the question being asked by Baby Boomers, the first generation to see the full benefit of extra time and better health and longevity, and Gen Xers, who are just now entering the halftime season.

Testimony
Kenneth Yeung: Pictures Saving Orphans

Kenneth's first-half career was in the retirement housing industry. He also operated a highly successful tea company in San Francisco, where the substantial profits from his company are invested in meeting the deepest needs of others, not his own comfort or material gain. Profits from the company have helped American families adopt Chinese children.

A picture can indeed speak a thousand words, but for Kenneth, it was the words on a poster featuring the photo of a young Chinese girl that spoke to his very soul: "Priority – A hundred years from now it will not matter what my bank account was, the sort of house I lived in, or the kind of car I drove. But the world may be different because I was important in the life of a child."

A native of the Shantou, Guang Dong province of China, Kenneth understands more than most the meaning behind that message. Political oppression forced his mother to send him to live with relatives in Hong Kong, where he struggled with language and cultural differences, as well as heart-wrenching homesickness. What 11-year-old wouldn't be homesick?

Fortunately, caring neighbors reached out to boost him over the language hurdle and bridge the gap of his parentless childhood. "I learned early on in life that it is so important for someone to give you a helping hand if you don't have help from a family member," says Kenneth.

Several years later, an equally caring teacher started Kenneth on a spiritual journey. As he matured in his faith, one thing was certain: He wanted to help others as his way of giving back. He prayerfully contemplated a career in ministry or social work. "But God had different plans for my life," he says. "He led me to San Francisco, not into social work, but into business—and He expanded my influence far beyond what I could have ever imagined."

That business—a highly successful tea company—operates with an unwritten contract with God. "When I started the business," he says, "I told my Lord that I wanted to serve Him. 'This is your business. I am just your steward to manage it for you.' That unwritten contract guides how I treat my employees—and how I use the funds the business generates."

He first began by using profits to help hundreds of American families adopt Chinese children when no agency in America knew how to go about it. In 1993, Kenneth and his wife also adopted a Chinese baby, Melissa Joy.

A friend had asked him about his work with orphans. His eyes lit up and he simply said, "Would you like to see my photos? We built an orphanage in China." He reached down and pulled out a dog-eared little photo album and began to show him the most compelling shots of an orphanage for 100 little children, all of them disabled. Page 7 was a photo of him holding a little girl, and his friend was captivated by the smile on his face. "Who is this little girl," he asked, "and why are you smiling like that?" Kenneth told him her name and said, "I just paid to have her heart repaired. Without that, she would have been disposable."

In China, where baby girls are often abandoned, the opportunity to make a difference in the life of a child is great—so great that in 1995 Kenneth began an endeavor that took eight years to bring to fruition.

Considered an embarrassment to their families, the mentally and physically handicapped of China often are thrown into garbage bins. Burdened to make a home for these unwanted children, Kenneth negotiated patiently with the Chinese government. In November 2003, the Prince of Peace Children's Home (POPCH), located in the Wuqing district of Tianjin, opened its doors. Funded by the Prince of Peace Foundation and World Vision International as a joint venture with the Civil Affairs Bureau of Wuqing, the facility accommodates 100 mentally and physically handicapped children under age 6 and provides rehabilitation services to other disabled children in the province.

The home set a miraculous precedent in China: For the first time in history, the government had allowed a foreign organization to build, staff and manage an orphanage.

Today, highly trained staff and caring volunteers lovingly embrace children once viewed as society's trash—and they teach others to do the same. "I told the Chinese officials that we would not only build and manage the orphanage, but we would also set up a training center to help caretakers from other orphanages in China," Kenneth says. "What the Chinese government really needs is to see a model that an overseas Christian organization can come in and build this type of thing with love and care. I told the officials that God has loved us, and we want to share our love with the children in China. They accepted that. They even allowed us to engrave a Bible verse on the cornerstone of the building."

While he was going through the Halftime Institute, Kenneth's Halftime Coach asked him if he left any other passions behind during his first-half pursuit of success. After just a few seconds he said, "Well, yes, there is. I am very good at photography. I love photography, but about 15 years ago I gave it up because my business was growing and my family was busy."

Kenneth shared with his peers a plan for his second half of life. "I came to this day thinking I would sell my business and go to seminary and go into ministry," he said, "but I'm a tea guy—this is what I do and I am good at it, and I make a lot of money doing it. So instead, I am going to hire someone to take some of my responsibilities in my company, and I will go and capture the most compelling photos of disabled orphans in China to challenge others to help fund orphanages for these children—we'll even print them on the back of the tea packages we sell around the world. And I will go and ensure they are run well."

And that is what he is doing. His photographs represent the convergence of his passions: Tea company profits, compelling photographs, and disabled orphans who know everyday that someone loves them dearly. He recently won a prestigious award by the Chinese government for outstanding charitable organizations—the first non-Chinese citizen to receive the award.

Kenneth put it this way: "If I can help change the fate of a needy child, I'd rather do that than have all the world's luxury.

❓ *Points to Ponder*

1. For what great second half adventures has your life's first half prepared you?

2. What can you do now better than you ever could before?

3. How do you define success?

4. How do you define significance?

5. Is the best behind you or ahead of you?

➡ *Action Plan*

1. Read *Halftime* by Bob Buford.

2. Investigate resources on the Haftime.org website.

Write your unique action items in the spaces provided below:

3. _____

    _____

4. _____

    _____

5. _____

    _____

Chapter 9

Understanding Legacy

"The life of mortals is like grass, they flourish like a flower of the field; the wind blows over it and it is gone, and its place remembers it no more" (Psalm 103:15-16).

"If I leave my heirs all measure of gold and silver, and a wealth of earthly possessions, but no knowledge of Jesus Christ as Lord and Savior, I leave them nothing. If I leave my heirs no measure of gold and silver and no wealth of earthly possessions but a saving knowledge of Jesus Christ, I leave them everything."

—Alexander Hamilton

"Ever since I turned 65, I think a lot about how I am going to be remembered."

—Robert, a friend

"I have fought the good fight, I have finished the race, I have kept the faith" (2 Timothy 4:7).

"I want to leave my kids enough that they can do anything but not so much that they can do nothing."

—Warren Buffett

"There was a man who had worked all of his life and had saved all of his money.

"He was a real cheapskate when it came to his money. He loved money more than just about anything, and just before he died, he said to his wife, 'Now listen, when I die I want you to take all my money and place it in the casket with me, because I want to take all my money to the afterlife.'

"So, he got his wife to promise him with all her heart that when he died, she would put all the money in the casket with him. Then one day he died.

"He was stretched out in the casket; the wife was sitting there in black next to their best friend. When they finished the ceremony, just before the undertakers got ready to close the casket, the wife said, 'Wait a minute!'

"She had a shoebox with her, she came over with the box and placed it in the casket. Then the undertakers locked the casket and rolled it away.

"Her friend said, 'I hope you weren't crazy enough to put all that money in there with that stingy old man.'

"She said, 'Yes, I promised. I'm a good Christian, I can't lie. I promised him that I was to put that money in that casket with him.'

"'You mean to tell me you put every cent of his money in the casket with him?'

"'I sure did,' said the wife. 'I got it all together, put it into my account and I wrote him a check.'"

Sidebar

In his book, *The Angels Were Silent*, Max Lucado tells a story about getting on a commercial flight one evening. Taking his seat, he noticed that the man at the window has the most opulent plane seat he had ever seen! The seat was the most expensive leather, the armrest imbedded with jewels. His tray table was made of the finest mahogany. The seat included high tech custom lighting and a plasma TV screen. Max sat down and asked the man how he got such a luxurious seat. The man explained he bought it and paid for everything. He also explained that he intended to live on the plane and never get off!

The man with the plush seat was so caught up in his luxury that he forgot that this journey we are on is temporary and we all get off the plane someday.

All of us die. Our days are numbered. What we leave behind is our legacy. Our legacy is not random. We get to be the author of our own legacy!

We do have a financial legacy we leave behind. But that is only part of our legacy. Our reputation is part of our legacy. Our family is our biggest legacy. Did we leave them in a good place spiritually, emotionally and relationally as well as financially? True legacy planning takes all that into account. Many legacies fail because there was no intentionality about making it successful. We need to be intentional in preparing the next generation, communicating effectively and addressing relational issues.

There is a big difference between estate planning and legacy planning.

Estate Planning is:
- A death-related event.
- Transferring assets.
- Saving taxes.
- Guided by lawyers and accountants.
- Focused on money.

Legacy planning is:
- How we want to be remembered.
- Furthering Kingdom works inside the family as well as outside beyond our lifetime.
- Kingdom focused.
- Stewardship.
- Faith impact on heirs.
- Transferring values
- Wanting our financial legacy to advance our faith legacy and character legacy.

Special Guest
Legacy

Jay Link on Blessing (and not Cursing)
The Next Generation

Affluent parents know by experience that wealth is dangerous. There are real and serious dangers to heirs who gain access to unearned wealth. In God's economy there are spiritual and character-building benefits to working and being proactive. A person who has access to the wealth without having gone through the process of earning it runs huge developmental risks including:

- A lack of motivation to work
- A lack of perseverance
- Problems in relationships
- Struggle with self-worth
- Poor understanding of managing finances
- A sense of entitlement

Experience tells me that what most wealthy Christian families want for their heirs is not financial security but contentment, and those are very different things. Most of us would like for our children to have:

- Spiritual maturity – a healthy relationship with God
- Emotional maturity – a healthy view of ourselves
- Relational maturity – a healthy relationship with others
- Financial maturity – ability to handle money

These four maturities are the foundation upon which a successful financial legacy and wealth transfer are built. This is not a passive process. A wealth transfer plan should be created with these in mind and be intentional to reinforce and encourage those maturities and not impair and hinder them. The most important conversations about wealth and legacy do not occur in lawyers' or accountants' offices. They occur in your own living room. It is much more important to prepare your heirs than to prepare legal documents. The process of wealth transfer should begin while you are alive and able to engage and mentor and model to your children and grandchildren.

Special Guest: Ron Blue
The Six T's of Wealth Transfer

Transferring wealth is about more than transferring money. Effective biblical wealth transfer involved more than legal documents. The six essential decisions in the process are:

1. The Transfer Decision
2. The Treatment Decision
3. The Timing Decision
4. The Title Decision
5. Tools and Techniques
6. The Talk Decision

Let's take a deeper look at each.

1. **The Transfer Decision:** Everyone dies. Everyone will transfer their stuff to someone. There are no hearses pulling U-Haul trailers. When John D. Rockefeller, the richest man in the world, died, a reporter asked his accountant, "How much did John D. leave behind?" The accountant replied, "All of it!" The transfer decision includes who your heirs are and what you are leaving them. It also involves why you are leaving them (assets, legacy, reputation).

2. **The Treatment Decision:** Involves how you will treat your heirs. Most commonly, wealth transfer plans distribute to heirs in equal portions. But all children are not the same. Ideally in your wealth transfer you should love your children equally but treat them uniquely. A top priority should be how to best leave the wealth to the next generation in a way that serves God most impactfully. Some wealth transfer plans include leaving

substantial assets directly to grandchildren. Great care should be given not to usurp the parenting role of your children in your grandchildren's lives.

3. **The Timing Decision:** Thoughtful, prayerful attention needs to be paid to the "when" question of transferring. Financial wealth can be transferred while you are still alive, upon your death, or even delayed after your death to a designated time. The timing decision should be made with, once again, a focus on maximum Kingdom impact into the next generations. Ideally financial wealth will transfer after financial wisdom.

4. **Title Decision:** At the core of the "title" decision is to reinforce that what's passing is God's and the transfer is of temporary stewardship over God's wealth.

5. **Tools and Techniques:** This is the step where the normal documents come into the transfer process (wills, trusts, etc.) In the secular estate-planning process this is often the first step. But in biblical wealth transfer, there are four important steps that need to occur before the documents can be crafted.

6. **Talk Decision:** You should talk over your wealth transfer plan with your adult children. It should not come as a surprise to your heirs after death. It is unfair and unbiblical to leave an inheritance mess behind. The best approach to prepare your heirs is to personally communicate your plans to them so that you can explain your reasons and answer questions. There is no portion of your transfer that will be smoother with you out of the room than with you in the room.

The Talk about the distribution of your wealth might not be easy or comfortable, but it is inevitable that it will happen. The question is do you want to be in the room participating when it happens or do you want to be laying in a coffin in the front of the room while the conversation goes on without you! For more information see Ron's book, *Splitting Heirs*.

? Points to Ponder

1. How will your assets be distributed upon your death?

2. Who created that plan and what are the wealth values that drove the process?

3. Would someone reading your estate document be able to tell you are a follower of Jesus?

4. Besides financial wealth, what else is your legacy?

5. Is your legacy designed for financial impact or Kingdom impact?

→ Action Plan

1. Conduct a biblical review of our estate/legacy plan with a specialist in this area.

2. Read *Splitting Heirs* by Ron Blue.

Write your unique action items in the spaces provided below:

3. _____

   _____

4. _____

   _____

5. _____

_____

Appendix

Our friends at the National Christian Foundation have created a process to identify where you are on your giving journey. The questionnaire is included at the end of this chapter. These questions will help you identify which of the four giving stages you are in:

Stage 1: Emerging Givers

Are first realizing that their faith has a lot to say about money. Their personal gift of generosity is in its infancy. Giving is reactive, emotional and non-strategic, and emerging givers sense a real conflict between their desires for material things and the act of being a giver.

Stage 2: Maturing Givers

Realize that God not only has something to say about money in general, but about their money personally. They are beginning to seek out a biblical basis for their personal finances. They are beginning to seek God's purpose in their giving and are being more strategic.

Stage 3: Generous Givers

Are beginning to realize that all they have comes from God and He has entrusted them with wealth for a Kingdom purpose. They are moving beyond formulas, are being motivated by others and have begun to follow a Holy Spirit-led strategy for their giving.

Stage 4: Giving Advocates

Are seasoned, longtime generous givers who have learned and grown on their generosity journey and are actively sharing their experiences and resources to encourage others along their generosity journey.

Giving Journey Assessment

Where are you on your giving journey? This assessment tool can help you identify where you are on your journey.

1. **What motivates your giving?**
   a. A desire to help others, reduce taxes or to receive public recognition.
   b. A growing desire to give as you further understand God's plan.
   c. A desire to make an outward material expression of your spiritual commitment.
   d. A desire to show others how to begin their own giving journeys.

2. **How do you decide where to give?**
   a. Gifts tend to be reactive and directed largely towards those who ask.
   b. Giving is generally focused towards causes or issues that appeal to me.
   c. Gifts are made intentionally and aggressively to specific causes and organizations for which God has instilled a passion in me.
   d. In addition to other regular gifts, I make gifts designed to help others pursue greater generosity.

3. **What is your view of stewardship?**
   a. I believe my money is mine to spend and invest.
   b. I am beginning to understand that everything belongs to God and that I simply steward His assets.
   c. I view all income and assets in my possession as God's and attempt to use them all as He directs.
   d. I experience the blessing of generosity and of being a "cheerful giver"—giving brings me joy.

4. *How do you decide how much to spend on lifestyle?*
   a. Lifestyle spending tends to match my income—as income increases, my standard of living rises with it.
   b. I am beginning to contemplate the impact of lifestyle decisions; I may intentionally limit lifestyle spending in order to increase giving.
   c. My top priority is using my finances for Kingdom purposes, not enhancing my lifestyle.
   d. Lifestyle spending is of minimal concern; I experience a sense of purpose and calling while encouraging others to be more generous.

5. *How do you approach estate issues or inheritance issues?*
   a. My primary desire is to maximize the amount of wealth passed to my children and family.
   b. I wrestle with competing desires: I would like to transfer wealth to my children but also want to give to Kingdom purposes.
   c. I see assets as a sacred trust and make family estate decisions based on a desire for intentional transfer of spiritual character and financial capital.
   d. I am more energized by helping others experience the joy of giving for themselves than by passing on wealth.

6. *Where do you look for advice when making financial decisions?*
   a. I follow the advice of trusted peers and advisors—but not necessarily the spiritual truth.
   b. I am open to spiritual truth and guidance from trusted advisors.
   c. I actively seek God's spiritual guidance for all giving matters.
   d. I am actively following God's plan for my finances and counsel others in areas of stewardship and giving.

Total the number of choices you made in each group:

____ If you answered "A" for 4-6 questions, you are most likely an Emerging Giver.

____ If you answered "B" for 4-6 questions, you are most likely a Maturing Giver.

____ If you answered "C" for 4-6 questions, you are most likely a Generous Giver.

____ If you answered "D" for 4-6 questions, you are most likely a Giving Advocate.

Once you have identified where you are on your giving journey, you can create a personal plan for your biblical generosity. You can use the best practices we have described. Teachings, peers, relationships and tools should all be shaped to your point on your journey.

Resources

1. *The Treasure Principle* by Randy Alcorn – book
2. *How to Be Rich* by Andy Stanley – YouTube video series and book
3. *Generous Living* by Ronald Blue – book
4. *Spiritual Thoughts on Material Things* by E.G. Jay Link – book
5. *The Purpose Driven Life* by Rick Warren – book
6. *God + Your Stuff* by Wesley K. Willmer – book
7. *Faith-Based Family Finances* by Ron Blue – book
8. Generous Giving website: www.generousgiving.com
9. National Christian Foundation website: www.ncfgiving.com
10. *To Whom Much is Given Much is Expected* by E.G. Jay Link – book
11. www.Womendoingwell.org
13. Orchard Alliance Foundation website: www.theorchard.org
14. Waterstone Foundation website: www.waterstone.org
15. *Family Money* by Terry Parker and David Wills – book
16. www.halftime.org website for more details
17. *Splitting Heirs* by Ronald Blue – book
18. The Gathering Orchard Group: www.orchardgroup.org
19. *The Generosity Bet* by Bill High – book
20. *Stories of the Generous Life* by Bill High – book
21. *Abundant* by Todd Harper – book